GE
BAYTRIPPER

GEORGIAN
BAYTRIPPER

Lynne Barnes

Recipes by
Keri Lockhart

Illustrations and maps by
Beverley Smith

The BOSTON
MILLS PRESS

ACKNOWLEDGMENTS

We would like to thank everybody who helped us over the years, who gave us great information, wonderful leads, and words of encouragement. We especially thank Jean Colbourn, who loaned us special books and didn't panic when we kept them for two years. You must have known they would come back to you.

Cataloging in Publication Data

Barnes, Lynne, 1957–
  Georgian Baytripper

Includes bibliographical references and
  index.
ISBN 1-55046-296-2

1. Georgian Bay Region (Ont.) – Tours.
2. Automobile travel – Ontario – Georgian
Bay Region – Guidebooks. 3. Bicycle
touring – Ontario – Georgian Bay Region –
Guidebooks. I. Roberts, Keri, 1961–   .
II. Title.

FC3095.G34B564 1999   917.13'18044
C99-930188-8   F1059.G3B27 1999

Published in 1999 by
BOSTON MILLS PRESS
132 Main Street
Erin, Ontario N0B 1T0
Tel 519-833-2407
Fax 519-833-2195
e-mail books@boston-mills.on.ca
www.boston-mills.on.ca

An affiliate of
STODDART PUBLISHING CO. LIMITED
34 Lesmill Road
Toronto, Ontario, Canada
M3B 2T6
Tel 416-445-3333
Fax 416-445-5967
e-mail gdsinc@genpub.com

Distributed in Canada by
General Distribution Services Limited
325 Humber College Boulevard
Toronto, Canada M9W 7C3
Orders 1-800-387-0141 Ontario &
  Quebec
Orders 1-800-387-0172 Ontario & other
  provinces
e-mail
  customer.xctvice@ccmailgw.genpub.com
EDI Canadian Telebook S1150391

Distributed in the United States by
General Distribution Services Inc.
85 River Rock Drive, Suite 202
Buffalo, New York 14207-2170
Toll-free 1-800-805-1083
Toll-free fax 1-800-481-6207
e-mail gdsinc@genpub.com
www.genpub.com
PUBNET 6307949

02 01 00 99   1 2 3 4 5

Text and cover design by Mary Firth
Cover art by Beverley Smith

Printed in Canada

Boston Mills Press gratefully acknowledges
the Canada Council for the Arts, the
Government of Canada through the Book
Publishing Industry Development
Program (BPIDP), and the Ontario Arts
Council for their support of our
publishing program.

CONTENTS

Chapter 5

Chapter 6

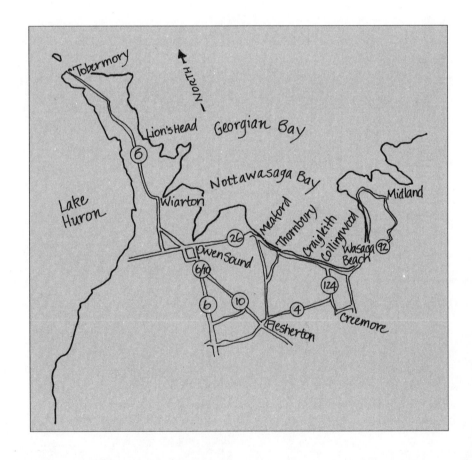

INTRODUCTION

GEORGIAN BAYTRIPPER IS OUR GUIDE to the backroads of southern Georgian Bay. Just what is a backroad? Most people see it as a dirt road leading to some unknown end. The Valley Girls, as we call ourselves, see things a little differently. For us, a backroad is any path or trail on which we can walk, ski, bike or drive. And even more, a backroad is an adventure. Something mysterious happens once you get off the main thoroughfares. Freedom, exhilaration and a certain wildness take hold of the soul.

Some of the trails we travel for hiking or cross-country skiing were once used by the Petun, Huron or Ojibwa as trading routes and paths to water or hunting. Others were used by the pioneers as they carved their way through the woods to new homes and journeyed to the nearest town for supplies. Not all the routes in this book have such lofty histories, but many do, including the Corduroy Road, parts of the Bruce Trail, the Old Mail Road and more.

Many of our backroads look as if they haven't changed a bit since they were built. They lead to little villages and settlements, hushed in rolling hills, almost begging not to be disturbed. We smile and wonder — Little Egypt, Dunedin, Rob Roy, Hurlburt's Landing — what histories do they conceal?

Lynne, Keri and Beverley, all longtime residents of the Thornbury area, have each enjoyed the backroads of the southern Georgian Bay region in different ways. Lynne loves to hop in the car and head down any road that sparks her interest, though she has been known to bike ride and hike too. Beverley has covered the backroads on cross-country skis by winter and bike by summer, but she knows her way up and down a backroad or two by car as well. Keri is the all-rounder, having taken advantage of all modes of transportation over the years.

The three of us decided to combine our mutual love of a good Georgian Baytrip with our other interests and talents to create this book. Lynne is the historian and writer, Beverley the illustrator, and Keri the chef supreme. *Georgian Baytripper* is a combination of three books we published between 1993 and 1995: *Daytrips on the Backroads, Daytrips on the Bike Trails* and *The Gastronomic Daytripper*. We've updated them, added cross-country skiing and hiking routes, a brief history of the native people of Georgian Bay, and a section on Midland.

Georgian Baytripper's maps and written directions make it easy to follow along. We suggest you read the text before departure and double-check the maps. Many of these routes can be travelled by mountain bike; others are recommended for road bikes. And don't forget to pack a fabulous picnic made from our scrumptious recipes.

We hope you enjoy.

Lynne Barnes, Keri Lockhart, Beverley Smith

The Rules of Backroading

1. Turn off your cell phone.

2. Do not ask for directions unless you are totally lost for more than 15 minutes, or you are in a state of total confusion, or you come upon a six-lane highway.

3. The backroads of Georgian Bay are skee-wonked in their angles. To make it easier to navigate, we'll call roads more or less parallel to the water east-west, and roads towards or away from the Bay, north-south. The exceptions are Tobermory and Midland (on the west and east sides of the Bay), which we will consider north. Clear?

4. Most routes can be used year-round.

5. Turn off the portable fax machine.

6. Have a picnic anytime and place, but please respect private property.

7. We trust our maps and written directions are clear. If not, see rule 2.

8. Ninety percent of the churches, schoolhouses, and other buildings in Beverley's illustrations are what you'll actually see. The other ten percent are imaginative composites; don't go crazy looking for them.

9. When driving on unpaved roads, pretend you are on ball bearings. Slow down, take turns with care, and pump the brakes. Take care passing slow-moving farm vehicles.

10. Fill your gas tank before leaving home.

11. Don't rush when backroading.

Picnic and Recipe Tips

THE RECIPES IN *GEORGIAN BAYTRIPPER* are an easy-to-make assortment of power snacks, picnic treats, dinner recipes, and wholesome food. Most recipes can be prepared the night before. To dine graciously and protect the beautiful landscape of Ontario, use silverware, napkins, unbreakable mugs and chinaware, and a Thermos or partially frozen plastic jug. Some recipes are made to travel well in a packsack. Many use honey instead of sugar for quick energy. Bring something to drink with you; not all villages have a general store. Whether driving, hiking or cycling, always remove your litter.

As you picnic or dine overlooking a panorama, perhaps you can imagine the efforts of early homesteaders, threshing wheat by hand, churning butter, and boiling down sap while trying to clear a plot of land from the forest. Many edibles such as maple syrup and whitefish are native to Grey and Bruce Counties. The European settlers introduced others — apples, cheese and butter. Some early foodstuffs were delicious, and some ingenious concoctions, such as beer made with spruce oil and molasses, were definitely an acquired taste. Choose your own feast for the road.

THE RULES OF BIKE TRAILS

WELCOME TO THE JOYS OF CYCLING in southern Georgian Bay. Today's lightweight bicycles, with narrow tires and many gears, are perfect for the paved secondary roads of Ontario. Hybrid and mountain bikes can traverse all road and trail conditions, be they gravel or cobblestone, field or stream, or rocky, rutted trails as primitive as those that challenged the early settlers. To enjoy cycling to the fullest, follow these simple rules.

1. Use only mountain, hybrid, and road bikes on these routes. No motorized vehicles off-road, please.

2. We recommend you read each chapter before heading out to familiarize yourself with the stories and plan your route and your breaks.

3. Remember the rules of the road. Ride on the right-hand side, ride single file, keep both hands on the handlebars, and watch out for traffic.

4. Stay on the trail or road to protect the flora and fauna.

CHAPTER 1

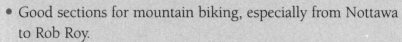

- Excellent drive.
- Good sections for mountain biking, especially from Nottawa to Rob Roy.
- Great hiking; look for the Bruce Trail markers.

Our journey into the past begins on Nottawasaga Sideroad 30-31, located across from the Emanuel Presbyterian Church about 2 kilometers south of Nottawa. Turn west off Highway 124.

Nottawasaga Sideroad 30-31 did not exist when the first pioneer families settled in Rob Roy. In all likelihood, they trudged for hours through a vast uncut forest, ill equipped, improperly dressed and weighed down with necessary supplies. Wolves and bears lurked in the thick growth. Roots and rocks twisted unsuspecting ankles. Unforeseen streams had to be forded. The settlers' lack of knowledge of their new land was the greatest danger of all. With only the blue sky above for comfort, 19th-century Ontario was a strange and frightening paradise.

As Collingwood grew, more families settled in the surrounding lands. Men journeying to Collingwood and back with supplies created crude trails. The paths of least resistance were, of course, the most travelled. These eventually became the surveyed routes and, later, today's roads. Perhaps this is how Sideroad 30-31 came into existence.

- **Great view.** About 4 kilometers west of Highway 124 on Nottawasaga Sideroad 30-31, look for a short, sharply sloping hill. From here, the Bay shimmers in the distance and the hills curve gently to the west.

Back on the road, continue west to the first village of our exploration. Rob Roy was named for the Scottish Highland clan chief Rob Roy MacGregor, who, like Robin Hood, has become idealized over the centuries.

The Krebs family first settled here in the mid-1800s and, for a time, were the sole residents. Enough weary travellers passed through each month to warrant the Kreb's opening of a public house that combined inn, tavern and . . . church! The public house no longer exists today, but the schoolhouse, still standing at the crossroads, is testament to Rob Roy's eventual status as a full-fledged community.

At the Stop by the schoolhouse, turn west onto Grey Road 31.

- **Look for Aqua Farms on the map.**

Most of Grey Road 31 is swamps, cedars and rugged marshland. You may well wonder how anyone eked out a life here during the last century. A few toughed it out, establishing the Methodist church and cemetery on the south side of the road. The church building is dated 1892. Perhaps an earlier church may have been in a settler's home: some of the gravestones date back to 1862.

One tall old gravestone near the road is particularly poignant. A wedding photograph on the stone shows a happy young bride and groom proudly posing for the camera. The dates indicate the bride passed away soon after.

At the Stop sign just after the church, turn south on Grey Road 2 and follow it until you find Osprey Township Concession 8 & 9 (just before the bridge into Feversham). Turn west here.

- **Look on the map for the Feversham Gorge.** It's a good picnic spot with parking and facilities.

Osprey Township Concession 8 & 9 is a peaceful, straight stretch of road with some surprise twists. Keep an eye on the south side for a tiny stone house with green awnings. Even though the

14

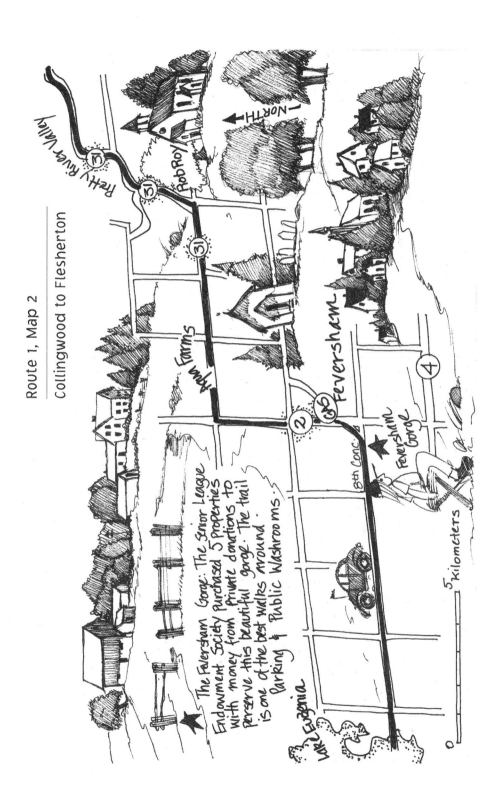

Route 1, Map 2

Collingwood to Flesherton

Pretty River Valley

RobRoy

NORTH

Abbey Farms

Feversham

Lake Eugenia

8th Conc.

Feversham Gorge

The Feversham Gorge: The Senior League Endowment Society purchased 5 properties with money from private donations to preserve this beautiful gorge. The trail is one of the best walks around. Parking & Public Washrooms.

5 kilometers

0

15

Burns moved long ago, this land is still known locally as the Burns' Farm.

The land was originally settled as a Crown grant in the 1850s and was eventually sold to Mr. Burns. Burns promised to place a landmark on both the east and west sections of his land. He constructed his main house around the corner from where you are now. He started work on the little house with the green awning, his landmark for the east, building it by hand and hewing the shingles himself, but the project was never completed and no one seems to know what became of Mr. Burns.

As you continue west, picture these lands in prehistoric times. It is 9000 BC. The massive, frozen sheet of the ice age is beginning to recede, and glacial Lake Algonquin lies just to the north. The southern shoreline runs along the top of today's Niagara Escarpment and the northern shoreline is a massive sheet of ice.

The Fluted Point People live and hunt in this cold land. Dressed in clothing made from hides and fur, hunters bring down mammoth and mastodon using chipped-stone spearheads with shafts made from the bones of those very animals. The Fluted Point People also consume bison, caribou, small animals and plants.

As the glaciers melt further and the climate warms, the land changes. The Lichen Woodland, with its open spruce forests, grass and sedges, gives way to the Boreal Forest. The forest grows dense with jack pine and birch. Grasses and lichen, the main food source for the mammoth and mastodon, begin to disappear. By 2000 BC, these two great Pleistocene mammals have been starved and hunted into extinction.

The Fluted Point People, however, survive and adapt. Over a 5,000-year period, they learn new methods of weapon- and tool-making. Other cultures from the west and the south make contact. Trading goods and ideas advances each culture.

By 1000 BC, water levels reach those we know today. The land is covered with familiar trees and plantlife — white pine and birch, elm, oak and maple, hemlock, beech, grass and ragweed. The people in these forests make fine tools and weapons, pottery and pipes.

With the emergence of the Iroquois people came the introduction of corn agriculture to Southern Ontario around AD 500. The Iroquois eventually occupy lands stretching from the south shore of the St. Lawrence, across Upper New York State to Lake Erie, and northward to the southern and eastern shores of Georgian Bay where the Petun and the Huron come to live. To the north and east of these two Iroquois nations, occupying an enormous area of land, were Algonkian-speaking nations, including the Ojibwa and the Ottawa.

Back in the car, on Concession 8 & 9, we begin a slow ascent. Over the crest of this long hill lies the fascinating and surprising Lake Eugenia, with its long causeway and vast lake on either side.

There was great controversy when Lake Eugenia was created in the early 1900s to harness the power of hydro electricity, primarily

to supply energy to the fast-growing city of Toronto. First, 1,900 acres of farmland were bought up, and houses dismantled and moved or simply torn down. Then the waters of the Beaver and Little Beaver Rivers were diverted to flow into the east end of the property and a dam was built to the west. By 1915, once the acres of farmland were flooded, the water flowed under the dam and into penstocks built into tunnels, and the Lake Eugenia site was created.

Stay on Concession 8 & 9 until you reach the T at Grey Road 13, the Valley Road. The village of Eugenia is to the north, but you will have to head south on Grey Road 13 to complete the journey.

- **The road to Flesherton, Grey Road 13, is perfect for cyclists.**
- **Look on the map for Eugenia Falls, a conservation area great for short hikes and picnics.**

Lake Eugenia was named for the nearby village of Eugenia, established before the lake was created. Two young French soldiers employed by Charles Rankin to survey the area suggested the settlement be named for Princess Eugenie, wife of Napoleon III.

Eugenia was the sight of a mini-goldrush in 1853 soon after a fellow named Brownlee was drawn to the area by the roar of falling water. Brownlee discovered not only the now-famous Eugenia Falls but the glint of gold as well. One way or another, word of the precious find brought many fortune hunters to Eugenia. When Brownlee went to New York to have the golden metal tested, however, he learned he had only found iron pyrites — fool's gold.

Follow the conservation area signs along a short hike to see beautiful Eugenia Falls, one of the seven ancient wonders of Grey County.

Grey Road 13 continues south to Highway 4. Turn west and follow Highway 4 to Flesherton.

Collingwood to Flesherton

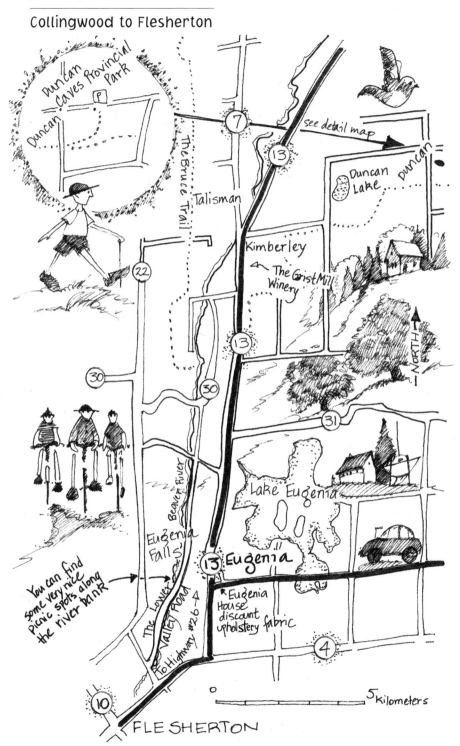

Duncan Caves Provincial Park

Duncan

P

The Bruce Trail

Talisman

7

13

see detail map

Duncan Lake

Duncan

Kimberley

The Grist Mill Winery

22

NORTH

13

30

30

31

Lake Eugenia

Beaver River

Eugenia Falls

You can find some very nice picnic spots along the river bank

The Lower Valley Road

To Highway #26

13 Eugenia

Eugenia House discount upholstery fabric

4

0   5 Kilometers

10

FLESHERTON

19

Route 2, Map 1

Thornbury and Meaford to Flesherton

ROUTE 2: THORNBURY AND MEAFORD TO FLESHERTON

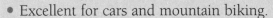

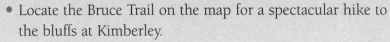

- Excellent for cars and mountain biking.
- Locate the Bruce Trail on the map for a spectacular hike to the bluffs at Kimberley.

Halfway between Thornbury and Meaford, you will find the Collingwood–St. Vincent Townline. Follow this road south as it veers away from the water. At the end of a long, climbing curve, jog left, or southeast and follow this road.

The Collingwood-St. Vincent Townline ascends steeply from the shores of the Bay, offering many interesting sights. As you round the first curve on the west you can glimpse Grand View Farms bison ranch.

About 5 kilometers in from Georgian Bay, on the plateau set high above the water, you will find Hurlburt's Landing, named for Heman Hurlburt who came here in the 1840s. Although an early settler, Mr. Hurlburt wasn't completely alone on his mountain, then known as the Blue Hill. Surveyor Charles Rankin lived just down the hill.

Mr. Rankin used his home at Lora Bay, then called Rankin's Landing, as his surveying base. He laid a narrow, primitive road along the shore of the Bay, a road that eventually became Highway 26. He probably marked a rudimentary pathway to divide Zero and Alta Townships. That division is the road upon which you now drive; Zero became St. Vincent Township, while Alta became Collingwood Township.

A mile or so south of Hurlburt's Landing, the Mackey family settled in 1835. Descendants of that family still live in the house their forefather built. Just before he passed away, grandson William "Bill" Mackey gave us a unique glimpse of the past with his tales of the Townline's settlers.

The first Mackey to settle here came from Barrie, where he officially received his grant of land from the Crown. He then walked 55 miles from Barrie to find his future. "His land, of course, was nothing but trees and rocks that had to be cleared." As Bill Mackey pointed out, "That doesn't happen overnight."

The closest supplies at this time came from Collingwood. That original Mr. Mackey began his gargantuan task by digging a small garden for those two basics of Ontario settlement, turnips and potatoes. After building a simple shelter, he cleared his 50 acres. "His plan was to raise cattle," Bill Mackey said. Generations later, cattle still graze the land.

Bill Mackey and his wife, Gert, lived in the home originally built by Russel McGuire, another early resident along the Townline. Mr. McGuire was the mailman. "He looked after the route for years. It covered the area from Barrie to Owen Sound and he looked after it all on foot," Bill Mackey said.

And what of Heman Hurlburt, the Mackey's neighbour along the trail? He planted one of the earliest apple orchards in the area, a crop that continues to be important to the local economy. An orchard still exists on the land Hurlburt planted.

Hurlburt's Landing itself eventually became a large enough community to sustain a church, since torn down, as well as a school and cemetery, still found on the west side of the road. All of this happened because Heman Hurlburt took a leading role in his community by donating the land on which these buildings sit and many hours of labour to build them.

- **Great view.** On the plateau at the top of the Collingwood-St. Vincent Townline, about 2 kilometers south of Highway 26, you'll see Georgian Bay sparkle and shine below. Beyond a long curving horseshoe of shoreline, Christian Island appears out of the distant blue.

Thornbury and Meaford to Flesherton

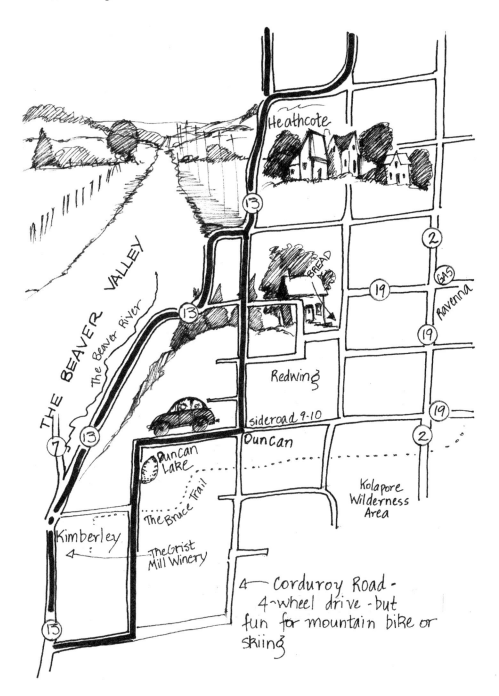

Heathcote

13

2

BREAD

19

GAS

Ravenna

THE BEAVER VALLEY

The Beaver River

13

19

19

Redwing

sideroad 9-10

2

Duncan

7   13

Duncan Lake

Kolapore Wilderness Area

The Bruce Trail

Kimberley

The Grist Mill Winery

Corduroy Road - 4-wheel drive - but fun for mountain bike or skiing

15

*Stay on the Townline until you reach Grey Road 13 at Heathcote.
Turn south onto Grey Road 13 and head into the village.*

Heathcote, or "Cottage in the Flat," was originally called
Williamstown after William Rorke. While not this settlement's first
resident, Mr. Rorke was perhaps its most influential. His log house
contained a general store and the only post office in Collingwood
and Euphrasia Townships. William Rorke was the village banker
and moneylender, the area's conveyancer, and the general agent for
deeds, mortgages and wills. He was council representative for
Collingwood Township and clerk for the united townships of
Collingwood and Euphrasia.

Just north of the village of Heathcote, on the east side of the
road, you will find a white wood-frame house built by William
Rorke and his son Thomas in 1853. This is the house from which
Mr. Rorke's many businesses operated, and Thomas continued
working here as postmaster until his death in 1900. The logs are
now covered over, but descendants of the Rorkes still own the
house today.

A trip to the village of Heathcote seems like a trip back to
William Rorke's time. Many families have been here for generations
and some buildings date from over a century ago. At the east end is

Thornbury and Meaford to Flesherton

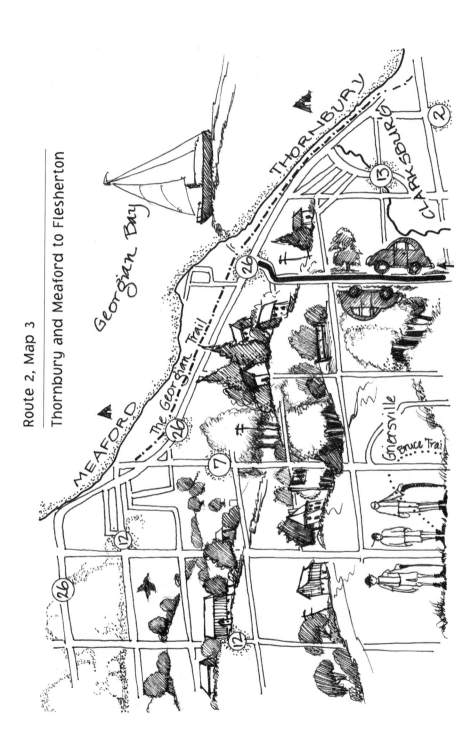

25

St. Augustine's Church, built in 1863 and now a private residence. On the south side of the main street you'll find a large building built in 1867 as Heathcote's "new" general store; it operated as such until well into the 1980s.

One other historical building is the Community Centre, which sits on the banks of the Beaver River at the bridge just north of town. Built as a meeting hall by the Society of Friends (the Quakers) in 1862, the Centre was moved to its present, beautiful location in 1910. The river widens out here and meanders beneath the shade of the willow trees, evoking days of church socials, box lunches and community picnics.

About 1.5 kilometers south of Heathcote, a sign points to Duncan. Turn here, onto the Euphrasia-Collingwood Townline, and follow it to the T-junction with Sideroad 9/10.

Like most settlements of the 1800s, Duncan was named after a prominent citizen, in this case, Duncan Boles, the first teacher in the settlement.

Let's sit on the Collingwood–Euphrasia Townline facing south at the T and take a look around this settlement. Across the road is a white house, formerly a post office and general store. The store began business in 1873 under the ownership of Alexander McKeown and was finally closed 102 years later by Alexander's granddaughter Grace Hindle.

Just down Sideroad 9/10, to your left, is Duncan Union Church. Now a private residence, the church was built in 1901 and acted as meeting place, social centre and church until 1965. In the field to the east of the Union Church once stood St. Alban's Anglican Church, an impressive redbrick structure with stained-glass windows and bell tower. This beautiful church was demolished in 1925.

Turn west at the T and follow Sideroad 10 around Duncan Lake to the T at Sideroad 100 and Grey Road 13, then turn north onto Grey Road 13.

- **Great view and picnic spot.** The lookout on the east side of Grey Road 13 provides an excellent view of the Beaver Valley. In October, the foliage is spectacular.

Follow Grey Road 13 to the bottom of the hill, to Grey Road 30. A sign directs you to the Beaver Valley Ski Club. Turn west (left) and follow the road past the ski club to where it makes a sharp turn to the west. Don't turn here, but go straight ahead onto the dirt road, called the Lower Valley Road. Follow this to the T at Highway 4. Turn west on Highway 4 and drive into Flesherton.

- **The Lower Valley Road,** one of the prettiest drives in the region, is excellent for mountain biking and picnics by the river. Railroad ties that sounded like xylophones when driven across once bridged many of the little creeks. The creeks still bubble musically through the culverts.

Established in 1851, Flesherton was known as Artemesia Corners until William Kingston Flesher came along. Mr. Flesher hired men to survey the area into lots for new settlers, thus creating a town he called Flesherton.

By 1883, Flesherton was a thriving village with sixty-four businesses, including mills, a printing office, an apiary, a cheese factory and even a photo gallery. Of the four general stores operating then, one, opened in 1867, is still in business. For today's traveller, Flesherton has antique shops, an "everything" store and an art gallery.

Residents of the town show great respect for their past by retaining the original look of the of the 19th-century buildings and lovely old homes that line the streets. Flesherton's best look at history comes with the Split Rail Festival held each September. Harking back to days of yore are competitions in log sawing and rail splitting. There's also a shingle-splitting display, horseshoe tournament, and quilt auction. At Split Rail time the community comes together to enjoy the company of neighbours and welcome visitors from near and far.

THE BRUCE TRAIL

THE GEORGIAN BAY AREA was once a vast wilderness. Signs of animal and human habitation were few and far between until the native population grew larger during the 1400s. A clearing might be cut here and there for a native village, but for the most part, the land was left alone. Those villages were often dismantled, and the land returned to its natural state. Later arrivals to this area found patches of second-growth forest that surprised them — until they learned more about their transient native neighbours.

To experience some sense of what this land looked like in the 1700s, try hiking sections of the Bruce Trail, developed in 1967 after seven years of planning. The Trail was blazed in the same way as the pioneers blazed theirs, marked by notches chopped into the bark of trees with a hatchet. The Trail's blazes (now painted onto trees, rocks and fence posts) are placed close together for hiker's safety and ease of travel. A turn in the path is marked with a double blaze. Blue blazes indicate the direction of water, a lookout, or a campsite.

From Niagara Falls to Tobermory, the Bruce Trail follows the Niagara Escarpment. The ancient rock found here was pushed up into the great wall it is today during the ice age some 10,000 years ago. Since then it has been constantly beautified by ice, wind and water.

The Bruce Trail supports 37 species of fern, 39 species of wild orchid, 53 species of mammal, and over 300 species of bird. You may see turkey vultures, hawks, the rare black-billed cuckoo, deer, porcupine, coyotes, and fox. Many plants and animals found along the Trail, such as the delicate and beautiful lady's-slipper, the Alaskan orchid, and the Massasauga rattler, are rare or endangered.

The Bruce Trail follows or crosses over many of the journeys you'll read about in Georgian Baytripper. Thanks should be given to those who use the trail, and the members of the many clubs of the Bruce Trail Association. In the area covered in this book, the Beaver Valley, Blue Mountain, Sydenham and Peninsula Bruce Trail Clubs maintain the trails and raise funds for its future. Without these clubs, we wouldn't have the Bruce Trail. Please help them by keeping the trail clean and stay on the marked path so you won't trample any delicate flora.

An Apple a Day

AN APPLE A DAY MAY KEEP THE DOCTOR AWAY, but where does all this preventative medicine come from? In this chapter you'll pass through hundreds of acres of orchard. Between Meaford and Collingwood are over 7,500 acres of apples, more than half located in and around the tiny towns of Thornbury and Clarksburg.

Knowledge of the apple has been with us for millennia. The crab apple, mother to all species, grew in prehistoric times. Evidence shows prehistoric man dried these apples and saved them for winter. The ancestral home of today's apple is probably the Caucasus. Many ancient methods developed for cultivation and storage of apples are still practised by today's farmers.

By the Middle Ages the French were championing the apple as a dessert fruit and had discovered techniques for growing a larger, redder product. The British, by comparison, simply made apple cider. With the emigration of the Huguenots, who fled France to practise their Protestant religion in Great Britain, apple cultivation knowledge eventually made it all the way to a location in the southern Georgian Bay area where a pair of well-placed natural wonders created a hospitable climate.

The cool waters of the Bay moderate seasonal temperatures, and the Niagara Escarpment acts as a barrier, or mini-ecosystem, to hold those temperatures. These two geographical quirks make Thornbury and the surrounding region a perfect place to grow two and a half million bushels annually.

The importance of the apple to the settlers of the area cannot be overstated; it was simply the best fruit for any pioneer to grow on his land. Apples grew easily, provided ample vitamin C, remained fresh for months when stored properly and were easily dried for use in the late winter months.

A settler's crop provided more than vitamins for his family. If he planted many trees, he could grow enough to make an annual trek to the nearest village, and sell or barter his produce for other supplies. Many early landowners planted at least one acre of apples. By the 1880s the apple business in southern Georgian Bay had . . . yes, had taken root. These days the apple still helps to feed and provide for many families in the area: a quarter of Ontario's apples are grown here each season.

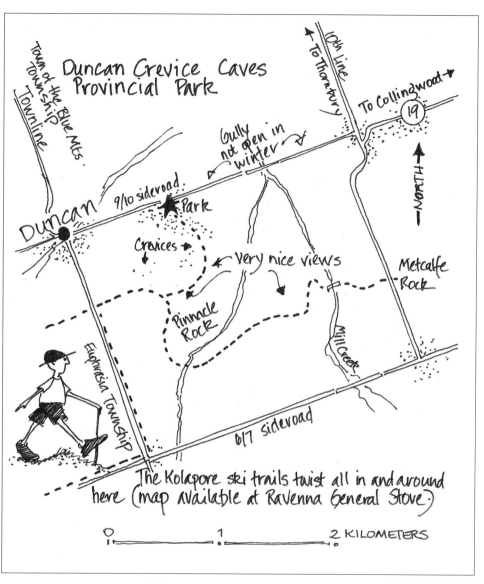

Detail from Route 1, Map 3, on page 19.

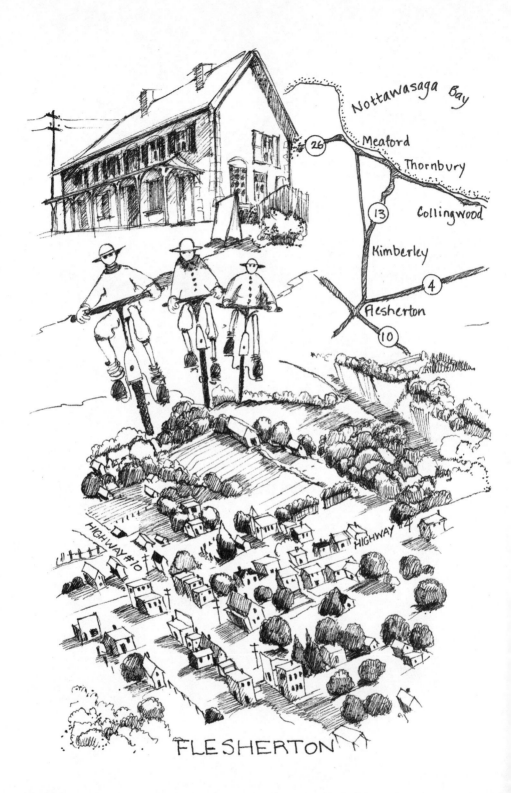

Nottawasaga Bay

26 Meaford

Thornbury

13 Collingwood

Kimberley

4

Flesherton

10

HIGHWAY #10

HIGHWAY 4

FLESHERTON

RECIPES

POTATO SALAD

BASIC RECIPE
2 lb. potatoes, cooked and diced
4 tbsp. mayonnaise (or 2 tbsp. yogurt
  and 2 tbsp. mayonnaise)
2 egg yolks, hard boiled and mashed
4 green onions, chopped
2 tbsp. olive oil
2 tbsp. vinegar

Add some (or all) of the following
  ingredients for pizzazz
4 tbsp. chopped gherkins

1 tbsp. capers
2 tsp. prepared mustard
2 tsp. chopped parsley
Celery, chopped
4 green apples
1 clove garlic
2 tsp. chopped dill
¾ lb (375 g) cold cooked beef, cut
  into strips
Spices to taste.

Cut the cooked potatoes into small cubes. Add all the basic ingredients and set aside.

Next, add in your choice of "pizzazz" ingredients to the basic recipe. Toss gently.

Salt and pepper to taste or, better yet, take salt and pepper shakers in your picnic hamper and let your guests help themselves.

Serves 4.

OVEN FRIED CHICKEN

1 cut-up chicken
1 egg
¼ cup milk
½–1 cup breadcrumbs or wheat
  germ

Seasonings
¼ tsp. garlic powder
Dash salt/pepper
¼ tsp. chili powder
¼ tsp. cayenne

Preheat oven to 400 F. Remove skin from chicken, if you like.

Mix egg and milk in bowl; mix bread crumbs and seasonings on a plate. Dip chicken in egg, then in crumbs.

Place chicken in baking pan. Bake for 1 hour, turning once with a fork.

Serves 4.

CARROT-APPLE SALAD

3 medium-sized carrots, shredded
  (2 cups)
1 large unpeeled apple, chopped
  (2 cups)
1 cup raisins
½ cup yogurt-honey dressing

Combine all ingredients.

YOGURT HONEY DRESSING

Stir 2 tbsp. honey into 1-cup container of plain low-fat yogurt. Serves 6.

MAPLE COCONUT SQUARES

1 ¼ cups all-purpose flour
¼ cup sugar
½ cup butter

1 ⅓ cups flaked unsweetened coconut
⅔ cup maple syrup

Combine flour and sugar. Cut in butter until mixture resembles fine crumbs. Press into an 8 x 8-inch baking pan. Bake at 375 F for 15–20 minutes.

Meanwhile, combine coconut and syrup in small saucepan. Cook, stirring constantly until coconut absorbs most of syrup, approximately 10 minutes.

Spread over warm shortbread base. Bake at 375 F for 10 minutes. Cool and cut into squares.
Makes 24 squares.

CRUNCHY APPLE CAKE

2 cups brown or demerara sugar
1 cup salad oil
2 eggs
2 cups flour
1 tsp. salt

1 tsp. cinnamon
1 tsp. soda
1 tsp. vanilla
½ cup chopped walnuts
3 cups raw apples, peeled

Cream sugar and eggs, and add oil. Mix all ingredients together (apples last). Pour into a well-greased pan and bake at 350 F for 1 hour.

GREEK SPINACH-CHEESE PIE

2 10-oz. bags of spinach
½ cup minced white onion
1 tbsp. olive oil
1 ½ tbsp. chopped fresh dill
2 dashes nutmeg
1 cup cottage or ricotta cheese

⅓ lb. crumbled feta cheese
2 spring onions, chopped
2 eggs, beaten
1 ½ cups wheat germ
1 ½ tbsp. melted butter

Wash and pick over spinach carefully; dry on paper towels, then chop.

Sauté onion in olive oil until transparent. Add spinach to onion, over and cook over low heat, stirring until most of the moisture has evaporated, about 8 minutes. Remove spinach from heat; add dill, nutmeg (salt and pepper to taste), cottage and feta cheese, onions and eggs. Mix well.

Combine wheat germ and melted butter; press into bottom and sides of a 9 x 9-inch baking dish. Pour spinach-cottage cheese mixture into baking dish and spread evenly.

Bake in preheated 350 F oven for 45 minutes or until crisp and brown. Slice and serve hot or cold.

Serves 4.

HONEY APPLE BROWNIES

2 tbsp. oil
¾ cup honey
1 beaten egg
½ cup applesauce
2 tsp. grated orange rind
½ tsp. vanilla

1 ¼ cup whole-wheat flour
1 tsp. baking powder
¼ tsp. soda
½ cup walnuts
½ cup chopped dates
1 tbsp. wheat germ

Combine oil, honey and egg and beat until fluffy. Add applesauce, orange rind and vanilla. Add sifted dry ingredients. Add dates and nuts.

Bake in 9 x 13-inch pan at 325 F for 20–25 minutes. Cut when cool.

Folk Medicine

To avoid colic for a year, on Easter morning, suck a raw egg laid on Good Friday.

To cure jaundice, eat carrots.

To ease rheumatism, carry a horse chestnut in your pocket.

For toothache, place a clove of garlic in the ear of the afflicted side.

To avoid toothache, have a child chew on a bread crust that has been nibbled by a mouse.

To lose warts, rub an apple slice over the wart while blowing on it. Another suggestion is to rub the wart with a piece of pork, which is then buried under the eaves. Or rub half a potato over the wart, and leave the potato in wrapped paper in a public place. The wart will transfer to whoever opens the package.

To cure a sore throat, tie a thin slice of well-peppered salt pork around your neck.

CHAPTER 2

ROUTE 3: COLLINGWOOD TO KIMBERLEY

- Good for cars.

This trip begins on 6th Street in Collingwood, then heads west towards the Stop sign at Osler Bluffs Road. Continue straight onto Sideroad 12-13.

- **For a pleasant hike,** look for the Bruce Trail where it crosses Sideroad 12-13 halfway between Osler Bluffs Road and Duncan.
- **Visit Bygone Days Farm** for its displays of original settler's homes, shops, churches and schools.

- **Great view.** This green and winding road is made all the more beautiful by its magnificent homes and spectacular scenery.

When Sideroad 12-13 ends at the T, turn south and follow the 4th Line for 1.5 kilometers to the Stop sign. Turn west onto Grey Road 19. Follow it to Grey Road 2, turn north here and continue for 1.7 kilometers. Turn to the west again, and follow this road, Sideroad 12/13, to the T and turn north on 10th Line into Redwing.

Redwing is a small village nestled between the protective arms of two steep hills. In 1849, the McColeman family built their home just south of the present village.

The brave spirit of Upper Canada's early settlers must have been doubled in those who settled Redwing. The place is isolated and the winters harsh. The two hills at either entrance to town present a challenge to today's vehicles, let alone yesterday's horse-drawn cutters and wagons. The homes, church and school built in the gully,

Route 3, Map 1

Collingwood to Kimberley

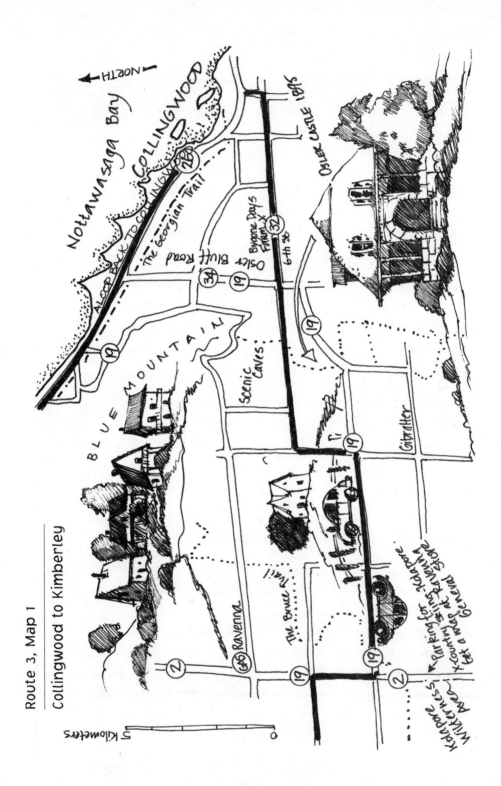

Collingwood to Kimberley

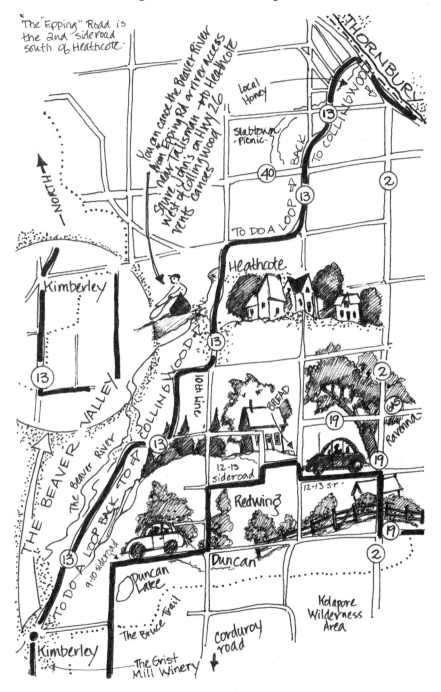

The "Epping" Road is the 2nd sideroad south of Heathcote.

You can canoe the Beaver River from Epping Rd. or river access near Talisman →to Heathcote. Squire John's on Hwy 26 west of Collingwood rents canoes

NORTH

Local Honey

Slabtown ~ Picnic

TO COLLINGWOOD

THORNBURY

BACK

TO DO A LOOP

TO DO A LOOP BACK

Heathcote

Kimberley

COLLINGWOOD

10th line

BREAD

12-13 sideroad

Redwing

12-13 S.T.

Ravenna

GAS

THE BEAVER VALLEY

The Beaver River

TO DO A LOOP BACK TO

9-10 sideroad

Duncan Lake

Duncan

Kolapore Wilderness Area

The Bruce Trail

Corduroy road

Kimberley

The Grist Mill Winery

on the hills and on the plateaus are testament to those hearty settlers who obviously could not be daunted by topography.

Picture Redwing in the late 1800s. You can see a furniture factory, closer to Mill Creek, a flour mill, a blacksmith's shop and, a general store and post office. Redwing is an active little community with businesses still operating in the gully and on the hill.

 • **Redwing Breadworks** is a great bakery.

In the gully in Redwing, turn west onto the 12th Sideroad and follow it to the T. Follow the road as it turns south and follow a slow bend west to the Stop sign. Turn south onto the Collingwood-Euphrasia Townline and drive to the next T. You're in Duncan. At the white house in Duncan, you have two choices, depending on your mode of travel and spirit of adventure.

The first is a pleasant drive and the easier journey for those who don't have a four-wheel drive or mountain bike, but it does skip Little Egypt. Turn west on the 10th Sideroad, then follow the road as it turns left on the 2nd Line, then right as the road now becomes the 3rd Sideroad. Follow this road to the T and head north down the big hill into the village of Kimberley.

If you're in a four-wheel drive or a very dependable car that can take a rough road, on a mountain bike, or looking for a good hike, turn east on Sideroad 9/10, then south on the Collingwood-Euphrasia Townline at the church (about 200 meters along the road.) At the crossroads of Sideroad 6/7 and Townline you'll find a No Exit sign. Ignore it and drive straight on the Townline.

This route takes you to Little Egypt, so named by George Teed in the late 1800s. Sensing ample food and prosperity, Mr. Teed took the name from the Biblical "There is corn in Egypt."

Never a full-fledged village, Little Egypt was still a solid community. Most settlers were farmers, but a small mill operated at one point as well as logging. Eventually enough families lived in Little Egypt that there was a need for a school.

The residents themselves decided on the site for their school-house, set the building budget, obtained the tenders and searched for their first teacher. In 1881 the 20-by-26-foot Union School Section 20 was completed and furnished, all for a mere 250 dollars.

This structure is proof that they just don't build things like they used to. It has been plastered then bricked over, left vacant for years at a time, served as a gun club, and moved twice, yet it still stands, as a private residence, on the west side of the road.

The bonds that tie a community such as Little Egypt together are difficult to break. In 1978 the new owner of U.S.S. 20 hosted a school reunion. Organized by the school's last teacher, who had taught from 1924 to 1941, the reunion attracted three other past teachers, as well as people from all over the region ranging in age from two to ninety-two. Many tales of the past were told as guests remembered times when the road was barely passable from December to April and days were spent clearing the land for farming. They spoke of bad times and good, and of all the elements that tie a community together.

At the junction of the left turn and the narrow straightway, continue on the straightway. This is the Corduroy Road.

- **The Corduroy Road** is excellent for hiking, mountain biking, and in winter, cross-country skiing.

The Corduroy Road is the greatest backroad in our book. This log road is the closest you'll come to the roads of a century ago. In washed-out areas, cedar logs poke out from the mud, perpendicular to the road, just as they have for the past 100 years or more.

Little information remains on this particular road. It's an old road, no longer used, with no official name. However, we can imagine how it was created. Kimberley had a flour mill and sundry other businesses, and was the only village in the area in which to pur-

chase supplies. Settlers from Little Egypt and surrounding communities such as Rockhaven, Little Germany and even Duncan needed to find the path of least resistance between their homes and the town.

In the 1800s, some settlers were paid four dollars per acre to clear the area roads and seed them with grasses. Livestock was then used to keep the grasses and weeds in check. Did cattle, horses, or sheep, once roam here? With the bluffs and Duncan Lake (then a swamp) between the settlers and Kimberley, perhaps they skirted these obstacles by this southwest route.

The settlers bumped along in wagons, an ox or horse hauling them. In late spring the ground was still swamped, with logs floating in the roadway. Supplies were always needed after a long, hard winter, however, and so they had to trust that the corduroy road would get them, albeit many hours later, to the newly cut and much improved Valley Road.

The Corduroy Road ends at the bend in the paved road, Sideroad 9/10. Go straight ahead, turn north onto Grey Road 13 at the T, and drive along it into Kimberley.

- **For a nice afternoon on the Beaver River,** canoes can be rented from Squire John's on Highway 26 between Collingwood and Thornbury. Canoe access is on Grey Road 13 just north of Kimberley, at the Water Access sign. For another access point, try the 19th Sideroad, two lines south of Heathcote. Because of dangerous debris and dams, do not canoe past Heathcote.

- **Fall colour tours.** Follow Grey Road 13 south from Kimberley to the lookout at the top of the hill on the west side. The contrast of the cold grey bluffs and fall colours is striking.

  Another choice for fall colour is to follow Grey Road 13 south from Kimberley, then turn west onto Grey Road 30, towards the Beaver Valley Ski Club. Go halfway up the hill and look back.

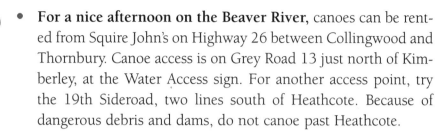

ROUTE 4: THE CORDUROY ROAD LOOP

- This 31-kilometer route is excellent for hiking, mountain biking, and cross-country skiing.

As you can tell by its name, the Corduroy Road Loop overlaps some of the area of the previous route, but there is much to know about this amazing little part of the world.

This route begins on the Osprey-Collingwood Townline, the southern border of a modern forest. (As the map for this route is so clear, we won't give you further directions.)

Route 4

The Corduroy Road Loop

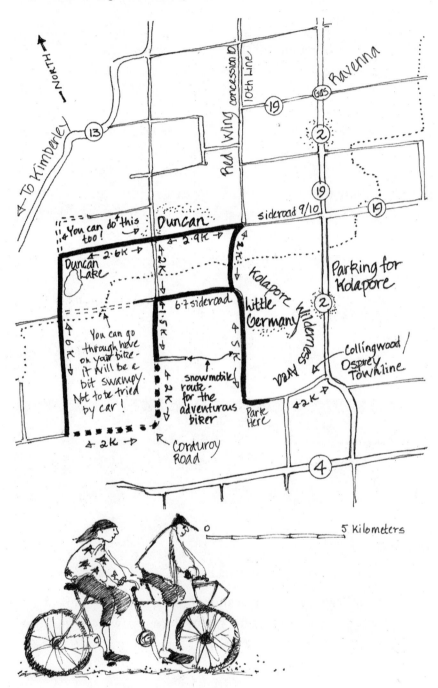

NORTH

To Kimberley

13

Red Wing concession 10

10th Line

Ravenna

19

905

2

19

sideroad 9/10

19

You can do this too!

Duncan

Duncan Lake

2.6K

2.9K

2K

2K

2K

Kolapore Wilderness Area

little Germany

Parking for Kolapore

2

6.7 sideroad

1.5K

5K

5K

You can go through here on your bike - it will be a bit swampy. Not to be tried by car!

snowmobile route for the adventurous biker

2K

Park Here

Collingwood / Osprey Townline

2K

2K

2K

Corduroy Road

4

0   5 Kilometers

44

Duncan Community

The Kolapore Forest belongs to the Ontario Ministry of Natural Resources. Thanks to modern management methods, the forest has grown into a fairy-tale "Emerald Forest," where the trees are so thick only mosses and ferns give the air within a hint of green. The same couldn't have been said in the past century.

Beginning in the late 1800s and continuing well into the 1900s, this forest was stripped of thousands of trees to supply lumber for building homes and ships. The heavy forest growth along these cross-country and hiking trails, once criss-crossed by logging roads, show just how forgiving Mother Nature can be.

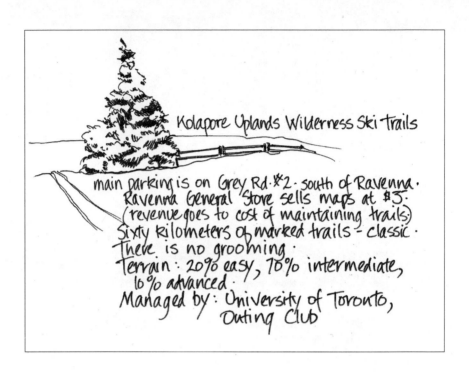

Kolapore Uplands Wilderness Ski Trails

main parking is on Grey Rd. #2. south of Ravenna.
Ravenna General Store sells maps at $5.
(revenue goes to cost of maintaining trails)
Sixty kilometers of marked trails - classic.
There is no grooming.
Terrain: 20% easy, 70% intermediate,
  16% advanced.
Managed by: University of Toronto,
            Outing Club

Ravenna General Store is a must stop, for not only do they pump gas and sell milk, they also are the local post office, bake bread, pies and buttertarts, carry local produce in season, homemade fudge, chicken pot pies, lasagna, fresh sandwiches, coffee, ice cream, designer children's wear, crafts, gifts, rubber boots, hardware, cross-country ski trail maps for Kolapore area, and they operate a bed and breakfast .... in other words... a true general store.

P.S. Very important for the daytripper - there is a phone booth outside the store and a johnny-on-the-spot kiddy corner to the store, in the public park.

- **Even the best navigators** would be wise to acquire a map for the Kolapore Forest. These can be purchased at the Ravenna General Store, 8 kilometers north on Grey Road 2.

After riding out of the Kolapore Forest onto the 6/7 Sideroad, you'll find a cleared section of road with cottages here and there, fencing, and a sign or two; you've come to *Little Germany*.

The first settlers arrived here in the 1870s, at a time when the industrial revolution was in full swing and the lumber business booming in Ontario. Immigrants who had once viewed the endless forests as daunting obstacles realized that a potential pathway to great wealth grew here.

Although thousands of board feet of lumber were being shipped overseas, Canada needed lumber for nationhood. Railways required thousands of ties, telegraph poles connected communities, villages expanded, and the lumber mills themselves used wood for fuel.

Lumber barons bought great tracts of land throughout Ontario, stripping their forests. Sawmills operated everywhere, including in Little Germany. The settlers here took advantage of the Kolapore Creek, building a shingle mill and two sawmills on its banks. Much of the land to the southwest was denuded to supply the mills.

And so the lumber barons took too much from the land. By 1900, they had depleted their wood supply. Villages such as Little Germany lost their main source of income. Hundreds of Ontario's sawmills and related industries shut down, leaving the villages that had grown around them to die. In our own backyards, we can ponder the rise and fall of history in such communities.

Two kilometers north of Little Germany on 10th Line, you'll come upon a small log house on the west side of the road. You are now in *Rockhaven*. This house belonged to the settlement's first pioneers, James and Joseph Bell, who arrived here in 1867, the year of Canada's Confederation.

The first sawmill began operation here in 1868, and by 1904, Rockhaven had two more sawmills and a short-lived creamery. A

There is a bridge just off the Beaver Valley Road, just south of Heathcote and each year it's neighbours put planters of petunias along the railing and it is always spectacular.

small train carried quarried rock to the many lime kilns situated along the base of the bluff where the rock was fired and used to make mortar. Now the University of Toronto Outdoors Club practises rock climbing on the great grey walls.

As you head west on Sideroad 9/10 through *Duncan*, look on the north side of the road for the Duncan Community Hall. This was once Euphrasia-Collingwood U.S.S. 16, the schoolhouse for area children from 1884 until 1968. The true spirit of this community, one of the few that actually own their old schoolhouse, can be found within the walls of this building. The people of Duncan still gather here to celebrate with costume and Christmas parties, potluck dinners and euchre tournaments, and to raise money for the upkeep of their former schoolhouse, now a modern-day community hall.

Every community has a story of life's seamier side. In *Little Egypt*, on the Collingwood-Euphrasia Townline, just south of Duncan, a pair of cousins ran their own "Country Club" businesses, inherited from their parents. From the 1940s into the 1980s, these Clubs were known far and wide by snowmobilers, hunters, cross-country skiers and anyone looking for a little fun. The fact that Thornbury was a dry town right into the 1970s helped attract a certain clientele.

To put it bluntly, the cousins were bootleggers. They did not brew their own liquor. They bought from the LCBO, which, rumour has it, delivered if the order was large enough. One cousin was known as the "legalized bootlegger." She refused to serve minors, didn't drink herself, and was known to physically remove any troublemakers with her own hands.

Inside, this cousin's house was dark and smoky. Her glasses were grimy, so smart customers drank beer straight from the bottle. Jokes and stories filled the air; people came and went; it was like any other bar . . . except it was illegal. Don't go looking for the cousins today, though you might find some obliging resident of Little Egypt willing to give you a drink . . . of water.

ROUTE 5: THE THORNBURY TO KIMBERLEY LOOP

- A 49-kilometer route for car or mountain biking.

From the community centre in Thornbury, head west on Alfred Street, turn left on Beaver Street, and follow the steep paved road. (This road, which is also Sideroad 33/34, was nicknamed "Frog's Hollow Road" after a long-vanished village.) Follow Frog's Hollow Road to Grey Road 7, then turn south to Griersville.

The Thornbury to Kimberley Loop

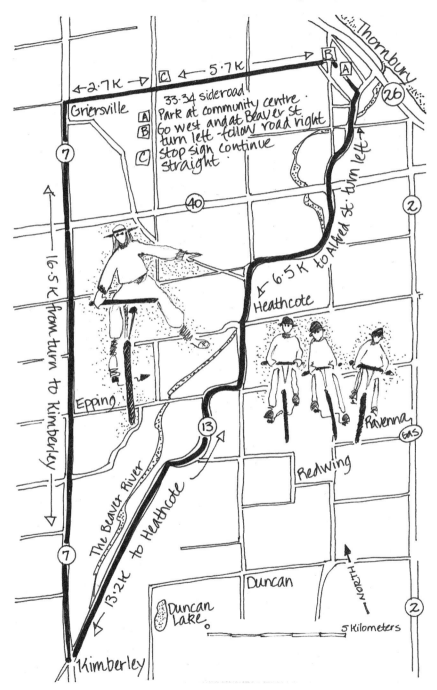

Thornbury

←2.7K→ C ← 5.7K → R
A
26

Griersville

33.34 sideroad
A Park at community centre
B Go west and at Beaver St
turn left - follow road right
C stop sign continue
straight

7

40

2

to Alfred St. turn left →

← 6.5 K to
Heathcote

16.5 K from turn to Kimberley

Epping

13

Ravenna
GAS

The Beaver River

← 13.2 K to Heathcote

Redwing

7

NORTH

Duncan

Duncan
Lake

5 Kilometers

2

Kimberley

• **Great view.** The Frog's Hollow Road has two steep hills. As a reward, when you get to the top of the second one, take the time to enjoy the panoramic view of the blue waters of the bay curving to the north and the green shades of the Escarpment sweeping south.

Once on Grey Road 7, having climbed yet another hill, you'll find yourself in the hamlet of *Griersville*, where a sign indicates the start of the legendary Old Mail Road. Most villages in Grey County exist because of the building of a mill or the opening of an inn or pub along a well-travelled route. Without the Old Mail Road, there may not have been a Griersville, nor a Heathcote, Ravenna or Rob Roy.

Also known as the Government Road and the Mountain Road, the Old Mail Road began life as a simple path through the forest from Duntroon to Rob Roy, northwest to Ravenna, then to Heathcote and on to Griersville.

By the 1830s, the Old Mail Road competed with the Lakeshore Road along the shore of the Bay. Nothing more than a rough trail, the Old Mail Road was briefly the main route for westward travel. This affected the settlement patterns of Collingwood, St. Vincent and Euphrasia Townships, as hundreds of settlers used the route. The government thought this the most sensible trail for their postal service and thus it earned its lasting name, the Old Mail Road.

 • **The Old Mail Road** makes a great hike. Keep in mind that you will be on private property at times, however.

Because the Old Mail Road passed through both Heathcote and Griersville, those towns became important centres in their respective townships. If we use the arrival of a post office or school as the benchmark for a community's coming of age, both villages were established ten to twelve years before today's better-known settlements of Craigleith, Thornbury and Clarksburg.

Situated at the west end of the Old Mail Road, Griersville quickly became the gateway to Meaford, Owen Sound and points further west. By 1845, a school had been built (across from where the present-day schoolhouse stands), and a short time later the general store, blacksmith, shoemaker, weaver and tavern made Griersville a bustling community.

An inn, with a tavern inside, stood on the northeast corner of Grey Road 7 and the Old Mail Road. As it was the only tavern for miles around, business was brisk. Legend claims the proprietor's two entrepreneurial children patiently waited beneath the porch steps, biding their time until some patron, having quenched his thirst a little too heartily, fell down the steps losing hat, pocket change and dignity. The children remained in their hiding spot until the gentleman had retrieved his hat and, brushing himself off, walked away. Then out they came to find all the pocket change left scattered in the dirt.

After the train came to Collingwood in 1855, the Lakeshore Road became the more sensible route for travellers and the mail. Craigleith and Thornbury blossomed as this more northerly road became well travelled. The Old Mail Road didn't quite fit the pattern of concessions and lines set out by government surveyors, nor had the government negotiated proper rights-of-way with landowners to continue using it as a mail route. Huge sections of the route grew over and, with that, Griersville lost its importance as a centre in the township.

This last vestige of the western end of the Old Mail Road, leading from Heathcote to Griersville, allows us to imagine those who travelled it through the isolated back country of the Townships. Those 5 miles of gravel, and their end, Griersville, make up a cherished piece of this area's history.

Continue south on Grey Road 7 downhill into Kimberley, and then turn northeast on Grey Road 13 to Thornbury.

• **Great view and picnic spot.** About 8 kilometers south of Griersville, watch the east side of the road for a gazebo, washrooms and picnic facilities at the Epping Lookout. This is one of the most beautiful views of the Beaver Valley.

LIFE IN THE CUCKOO VALLEY

MEMBERS OF THE PETUN NATION wintered under the protection of the Beaver Valley's bluffs beginning in the 1400s. They lived with the sounds of the wind rustling through the endless forest, the rush of the Beaver River as it surged northward, and the *coo-coo, coo-coo* of the cuckoo bird, so plentiful, the natives named it the Cuckoo Valley.

The Petun were related to the Iroquoian-speaking nations who inhabited a vast area of what is now known as New York State and the Great Lakes system. They included the Five Nations of the Iroquois, who lived by the southern shores of Lake Ontario, the Huron, who lived on the east shore of Georgian Bay, and the Petun, who lived on the southern shore of the Bay.

A peaceful people, the Petun excelled at trade and diplomacy. They had close links to their relatives to the northeast, the Huron, and became friendly with their neighbours to the northwest, the Algonkian-speaking Ottawa. The Petun made a habit of presenting gifts of meat and fish to guests, and their peace chiefs, or sachems, met annually with peace chiefs from unrelated tribes in order to exchange gifts at a huge feast during which speeches were made and the pipe was smoked.

These acts of friendliness served two purposes. First, they ensured peace throughout the nations and second, they ensured trade would continue among the tribes year after year.

By the mid- to late 1600s, however, peace no longer existed. The Five Nations Iroquois viciously attacked both the Huron and the Petun and diseases introduced by the coming of the Europeans also took their toll. The Petun were driven out of the area, heading south towards Detroit and the lands of the Cuckoo Valley sat silent for many winters.

Eventually, some tribes of the Ojibwa nation, relatives of the Ottawa, moved south to occupy the lands that include the Valley, and throughout the mid-1800s they became acquainted with a whole new tribe, the European settlers. Perhaps the legacy of those long ago acts of friendliness and diplomacy created the amicable atmosphere for these settlers and the Ojibwa. Many European settlers survived their first months in Canada because of the kindness of their native neighbours. The Ojibwa taught these settlers how to hunt and how to make maple syrup and gave needed advice on how to live in the wilderness. No stories exist of conflict between the two peoples who resided in and around the Cuckoo Valley.

Life was difficult for these settlers. Just battling against the currents of the Beaver River in bateaux and canoes to reach their lands was an arduous journey. Knowing they would be isolated, the pioneers timed their arrival so they could clear the land and plant for food well before winter. Running out of food during the winter could mean death for a family.

During the 1860s, however, life became a little easier for the people of what was by then called the Queen's Valley. The first flour mills in Euphrasia Township began operating, one of them in the newly developing village of Kimberley itself.

Another advance came with the building of the Valley Road (Grey Road 13) to connect two important existing roads, the Durham Road, which lay to the south of the growing village, and the Owen Sound to Collingwood Road to the north. A link between the two would benefit fledgling villages such as Thornbury, Clarksburg, Meaford and others, and it certainly established the Valley. With just minor variations, this road follows the route laid out by surveyor Thomas Donovan in the late 1850s.

The settlement at Kimberley became an important destination because of its flour mill, saw and shingle mills, general store, and school. In 1868, the postal station was named after the Earl of Kimberley, a British statesman.

The Kimberley of today isn't much larger than yesteryear's. Two of the old mills stand empty on the main street, but with Talisman ski resort nearby and the Bruce Trail across the bluffs, Kimberley is a busy and unique place. Because the Niagara Escarpment doubles back and enfolds the valley, no major highway was ever constructed. The valley has been declared an UNESCO Biosphere Reserve because of its unique geologic formations, microclimate, and unusual birds. In the forests of the surrounding valley, you might hear the *coo-coo*, *coo-coo* of the few black-billed cuckoo birds, living reminders of why this beautiful place was once called the Cuckoo Valley.

- **The 1877 Grist Mill Winery** on the east side of the main street of Kimberley is a great place to make your own wine.

- **Fall colour sites, great view, picnic, short hike.** For a great route for fall colours, follow Grey Road 13 north from Kimberley and turn east onto Sideroad 7B at the township store shed. Go up the steep winding road to the parking lot at the top and hike about 15 minutes up the well-marked Bruce Trail (here part of the Grey/Sauble Conservation Authority) to the top of Old Baldy. Another route follows Grey Road 13 south from Kimberley, then straight ahead on the dirt road, the beautiful Lower Valley Road, instead of around the bend and up the hill. A vista awaits around every curve.

Follow Grey Road 13 north out of Kimberley through Heathcote.

Now pass through Heathcote and the east end of the Old Mail Road. On the east side of Grey Road 13, you'll find a white, wood-frame house near the edge of the road. Opposite that house lies the Old Mail Road and, at the northwest corner of the intersection, the land that belonged to Heathcote's first settler, John Eaton.

Mr. Eaton built his log cabin near this corner in 1844. The Old Mail Road was a rough trail and travelling was arduous. Fortunately for weary travellers, Mr. Eaton recognized his isolated property was a perfect stopping point between Ravenna to the southeast and Griersville to the northwest. Mr. Eaton boarded many travellers, families included, for a night or two of rest.

Eventually this intersection boasted a post office, two stores, a tavern and the seat of government for the combined Collingwood–Euphrasia Townships' first Council. Boardwalks ran along the east side of Grey Road 13, and a school was built in 1868 at the bend just north of here. The schoolhouse still exists, but the Old Mail Road has disappeared.

Follow paved and winding Grey Road 13 to Clarksburg.

- **Great view and picnic spot.** Past the second bend after Heath-cote, you'll pass through a little community called Slabtown. From Grey Road 13, follow the road west (the one with all the mailboxes at the end) to the dam. Here you can go for a dip or just dangle your feet in the river, and relax.

The story of Clarksburg must be told through its first settlers, the Marsh family, and their home, Grape Grange. Built on the gentle slope just south of the hill into town, this home's golden brickwork, split-rail fences and majestic walnut trees make it a noteworthy property.

The roots of the Marsh family are as deeply embedded in Clarksburg's soil as are the roots of those walnut trees, planted by William Jabez Marsh, with the help of his young son, at the time he built Grape Grange in the 1850s.

Jabez was a farmer, a merchant and the founder of the Village of Clarksburg. When he brought his family here, Thornbury had a population of less than a hundred and Jabez and his wife had not one neighbour. The two of them came here, willing to start a new life and raise their nine children in the wilderness.

Jabez Marsh opened a general store in nearby Thornbury, commuting daily by horse or on foot, following a path he cut for himself. Meanwhile, Rosamund Marsh created such an air of welcome at their log home that it became a gathering place for friends and relatives alike. As Clarksburg grew, its residents enjoyed croquet parties, afternoon teas and summer picnics in the garden, while each Sunday afternoon they gathered at the house for church services.

The place was christened Grape Grange for the wild grapes that grow profusely on the property. Photographs from the early days show that, despite the brickwork covering the logs, Grape Grange is structurally the same home today as when Jabez Marsh built it in the 1850s. The bay windows and conservatory were added when the brickwork was done, but all changes have maintained the architectural integrity and living history of Grape Grange.

This beautiful home has stayed in the Marsh family since it was built, and it remains a gathering place for both friends and guests of this bed and breakfast. Its present owner, Nan Maitland, is caretaker of the family history. Surrounded by heirlooms, Nan recounts stories of the past. The young boy who held the walnut saplings straight while his father Jabez planted them was her grandfather, Charles Marsh.

Clarksburg grew into a quiet little village that maintains close ties with neighbouring Thornbury. Although the village took its name from its second resident, William Clark, who owned a woollen mill on the river, Jabez Marsh is fittingly remembered on the village's main street, Marsh Street.

 • **Great picnic spot by the river.** At the intersection at the bottom of the hill in Clarksburg, turn west off the main street (Marsh Street), pass the fire hall, and you'll find Fireman's Park on the south side.

Continue north from Clarksburg on Grey Road 13 (Marsh Street) and into Thornbury.

Long before apples grew here, the lands that now make up Thornbury were fertile. The waters of the ice age had subsided. The people who populated the vast continent had begun to make contact with each other, exchanging goods and knowledge. By around AD 500, one of the most important things the people of the northeast had learned from their neighbours to the south was how to grow corn.

As the Iroquois developed their agricultural skills, they cleared vast areas for villages and cornfields. Food gathering was a well-organized process for the Iroquois. The men hunted for meat while the women gathered berries and plants and cultivated the corn.

Members of each longhouse maintained their own fields and much corn was harvested for fresh use, dried for winter, and traded.

With corn the only crop, however, the soil was quickly depleted. Entire villages, from a hundred to as many as a thousand people, moved to new land. One fertile location was the Beaver River Delta near present-day Thornbury.

The present town of Thornbury was established as a town site during the early 1840s. In 1848 the first settler, Solomon Olmstead, built a sawmill, but it took a decade before anything resembling a town existed.

Thornbury has never looked back. With the coming of the train to Collingwood in 1855, the Lakeshore Road, until then a rough and barely trodden trail, became the main artery for travel to points west. With a good harbour at its north end as well, Thornbury blossomed. Soon it had three mills, Jabez Marsh's general store, four hotels, a blacksmith's shop and forty other businesses.

Let's go back to Thornbury in spring in the early 1900s. The snow is melting into the earth, making Bruce Street muddy and difficult. The warmth of April is in the air. Horses with buggies pass by with their drivers smiling proudly, nodding to an acquaintance here, and waving to a good friend there. For as long as good weather lasts, this will be a Saturday afternoon tradition. The boardwalks are busy with laughing children and adults. Nearly every hitching post has a horse patiently awaiting its owner.

The Thornbury of yesteryear isn't so unfamiliar. Many of the same businesses make up the main street, though in different buildings. There is a bakery on the southwest corner of the block, in a building that still stands today. A butcher's shop and a clothing store occupy the building that stands two north of today's post office. And the unique Ontario tradition of locating the coffin maker and funeral home next to the furniture store holds true. Yes, all are located in the huge building that today forms the southeast corner of the block.

Bruce Peninsula

Georgian Bay

Nottawasaga Bay

Owen Sound

Meaford   Thornbury

THORNBURY

In the alley behind the east side of the street, men stand in small clusters having a smoke and a "confab" before they hustle around to Bruce Street to see who they'll run into next.

The best way to imagine Thornbury's past is on foot. A stroll north on Bruce Street takes you to one of the loveliest harbours on Georgian Bay; a walk south takes you back in time. Many successful families settled in Thornbury, families who built gorgeous homes throughout the town. Some fine examples of architecture dating from the 1880s and into the 1900s can be seen in the first two blocks south of the business section. These homes belonged to the town's doctor, its banker, a lumber baron and other well-to-do families.

Also south on Bruce Street are its churches. The First Baptist Church, at the southwest corner of Bruce and Alice Street was built in 1907, and Grace United Church, found further along Bruce on the same side, was built in 1881.

Anyone who visits Thornbury immediately notices its friendly people. Thornbury is a great place on a Saturday afternoon for a slow walk down the main street and a "confab" with a friend or two.

ROUTE 6: A JOURNEY TO BADJEROS

- A 74-kilometer loop for car or mountain bike. See maps for added bike routes.

Start in Kimberley, head south on the Valley Road, Grey Road 13. Drive up the big hill to the junction of Valley Road and Highway 4, and turn east onto Highway 4.

- **Great view and picnic spot.** At the top of the big hill, rest at the Beaver Valley Lookout on the west side of Grey Road 13.

The writing on the saw-blade sign claims Rock Mills has a population of fourteen, but is "Still Growing." At its peak, a whopping

Route 6

A Journey to Badjeros

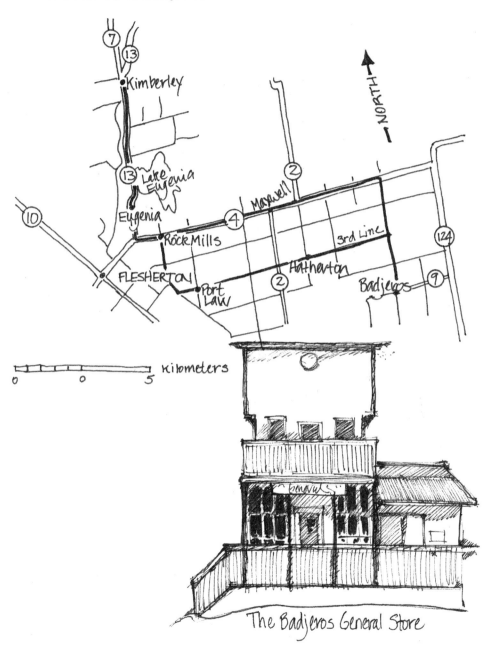

The Badjeros General Store

thirty people resided here, most employed by the mill that gave the settlement its name.

For close to fifty years, that sawmill dominated life in this area. In Rock Mills, many families lived in houses built by the mill. The large grey Insulbrick building near the intersection was a company house for single men.

Further from the settlement, farmers trusted the shrill sound of the mill's whistle to guide them through the day. With the 7 a.m. whistle, work commenced. The noon whistle sent them home for a hearty dinner and an hour later returned them to the fields. The final whistle ended the mill workers' day at 5 p.m. The farmers, however, ignored this whistle, working till dark to finish their long day's work.

In the early 1950s the sawmill closed and many families moved away from Rock Mills. The mill was torn down, leaving only the saw blade as its legacy. Listen closely and you may hear the faint sound of the whistle in the air.

Continue east on Highway 4.

Highway 4 was once called the Durham Road; it is one of southern Georgian Bay's oldest thoroughfares. Heavy use of this road made the village of Maxwell the hub of Georgian Bay's grain industry from 1860 to 1865.

Wagons came by the hundreds, loaded down with grain to be weighed and sold. Moved onto yesteryear's version of a transport truck — a huge wagon hauled by a large team of horses — the grain was driven east on the Durham Road, then north to Collingwood. From there, the cargo shipped out by rail or ship. From 1863 to 1864, 32,000 bushels of grain were sold out of Maxwell.

With all of this activity, Maxwell became a well-established village. Besides the weighing stations and other related businesses, there was a blacksmith, a shoemaker, a carpenter, a cabinetmaker, a church and school, and a hotel owned by Joseph Maxwell, for whom the village is named.

- **On the south side of the road is an emu farm.** These large, flightless birds, second in size only to the ostrich, are one of Ontario's newest variety of livestock. They wander close to the road, but don't try to touch them. At the farm, you can buy a range of emu products.

Continue east on Highway 4 to Osprey 60, to the Badjeros sign, and turn south onto Osprey 60 to Badjeros.

Along the way to Badjeros, you'll pass a crossroads settlement called McIntyre, named for the four brothers McIntyre who took up residence there, each on a corner of the crossroads. At the intersection, look east for the peaked roof of the McIntyre United Church, a lovely little building with gingerbread trim. Its stone marker, dated 1879, has been worn by time and the winds of Osprey Township until the numbers are barely visible. A look west shows the Pioneer Cemetery, established in 1854. In nearly all of the graves rest brave settlers of the 1800s, their worn and crumbling headstones leaning in all directions.

The general store, with its beautiful architecture and the large porch painted bright red, is the first thing you'll notice in Badjeros (accent on the first syllable, pronounce the *j*). Dating from the 1880s, the store stocks everything from rubber boots to candy, flannel shirts to shoe polish, canned goods to videos. Even the post office operates from here, with the store's owner doubling as postmaster.

The man who built this lovely structure was Neil D. McKinnon, proprietor until 1904 when he sold the business and moved west. Let's visit Mr. McKinnon to experience an ordinary day in a general store typical of the many you'll come across in this part of the world.

You eagerly climb the stairs Badjeros General Store to catch up on the news with the customers within. The hours on the sign at the entrance read "Monday to Friday 7 a.m. to 7 p.m., Saturday 7 a.m. to 10 p.m." Mr. McKinnon is in his shop every hour it is open. When does he do his accounting?

Nearly everything you need can be found in this place, and you've come armed with your list. You scoop some basics, flour and cornmeal, from the bulk bins into paper sacks. You put a few other items — lamp oil, screws and nails, a pair of pants and yet more food items — on the counter.

Mr. McKinnon adds up the bill. Eggs are one cent each, butter twenty-five cents a pound, beef is fifteen cents a pound, the loaf of bread is five cents, and a ninety-pound bag of potatoes costs you fifty cents. You trade milk from your farm for two rather extravagant purchases, sugar and a bit of spice.

Mr. McKinnon wraps the butter, meat, eggs and other items in paper, then knots it with string, thanks you cordially and moves on to the next customer. His work never stops. Maybe that explains his departure west.

It was not uncommon for a turn-of-the-century Osprey Township settler to heed the call to head west. High on a plateau, the area sustains long winters with early frosts and late springs. Crops were destroyed by this climate. Families ran out of food in the winter. In spring, hungry and weak, settlers had to clear more land and hope they could grow a big enough crop.

Although most of the Township's settlers were experienced pioneers, this area was too harsh for them. The proof is in the numbers. In 1882, the population of Osprey Township peaked at 4,000. By 1952, it had dropped dramatically to 1,760 and remains practically the same today.

On the south side of the road looking west, you'll find the village cemetery. A tavern owner named Phillip Badjeros donated the land to the village.

Return the way you came, starting on Osprey 60.

RECIPES

WHITEFISH

1 whole whitefish cleaned
   (about 2 lbs)
1 tsp. salt
4 slices lemon, halved

4 slices of onion
Pepper
1 tbsp. butter

Rinse fish, pat dry. Using scissors, remove fins and trim tail. Remove head by slicing firmly through backbone. Using sharp knife, cut diagonal scores about 4 inches long and 2 inches apart on each side of fish.

Place fish on a large piece of foil. Place lemon and onions, salt and pepper and butter on fish. Wrap fish tightly in foil.

Grill on barbecue 4–6 inches from flame on medium-high setting. Grill fish for 10 minutes per inch of thickness or until flesh is opaque and flakes easily when tested with fork. Turn fish over halfway through cooking time.

Carefully transfer fish to serving platter.

Serves 4.

RICE PILAF

½ cup chopped onion
1 clove garlic, minced
1 cup raw brown rice
2–4 tbsp. oil
2 ½ to 3 cups liquid (stock, broth,
   water with 1 tbsp. tamari soy
   sauce, or tomato juice)

1 tsp. each of ground cumin and
   curry
½ to 2 cups sliced vegetables
   (mushrooms, celery, sprouts etc.)

Brown onion, garlic, rice and vegetables in oil. Add liquid and spices. Bring to a boil. Simmer, covered, until liquid is absorbed, 40 to 60 minutes.

This is a nice a side dish. Make it a high-protein meal by adding beans, hard-cooked eggs, cheddar, almonds or seeds.

WILTED SPINACH SALAD

16 cups loosely packed trimmed
  spinach
Half red onion, thinly sliced
1 cup croutons
1/4 cup toasted slivered almonds

1/3 cup olive oil
1/4 cup raisins
1/4 cup red wine vinegar
Salt and pepper
1 clove garlic, minced

Tear spinach into bite-size pieces; place in salad bowl. Sprinkle with onion, croutons and almonds.

In a saucepan, heat oil, raisins and vinegar over medium-high heat for 1 to 2 minutes or until hot; whisk in salt, pepper and garlic. Toss with spinach mixture. Serve immediately.

Serves 4.

CUCUMBER SALAD WITH DILL

1 English cucumber, thinly sliced
1/2 sweet white onion, very thinly
  sliced
1 tsp. dried dill (or more)
Salt and pepper

1 tbsp. honey, slightly warmed
1 tbsp. vinegar
1 tbsp. oil
1 cup light plain yogurt

Thinly slice vegetables, then add dill. Mix honey, vinegar and oil together and pour on vegetables. Refrigerate for one hour. Drain.

Add 1 cup of yogurt and salt and pepper to taste. A wonderfully cool, light salad.

HONEY FRUIT CRISP

6 cups sliced fruit (your choice)
1 tbsp. lemon juice
1/2 cup honey
1/3 cup unbleached white flour

2/3 cup rolled oats
1/2 cup brown sugar
1/3 cup butter

Arrange fruit in greased baking dish and sprinkle with lemon juice. Spread honey over fruit. Mix dry ingredients. Cut in butter until mixture resembles coarse bread crumbs. Sprinkle over fruit. Bake at 375 F until fruit is tender and crust is browned (about 30 minutes).

Serves 6.

RASPBERRY SQUARES

½ cup butter, softened   1 cup unbleached white flour
½ cup honey   ½ cup whole wheat flour

Preheat oven to 350 F.

Cream together butter and honey until light and fluffy. Add flours and blend well. Spread in an oiled 9 x 9-inch square pan and bake about 20 minutes until firm and just beginning to brown.

Cool 5 minutes before adding top layer.

TOP LAYER
1 ⅓ cups flaked coconut
1 cup raspberries

While cookie base is baking, heat raspberries in a saucepan until they become liquid. Add coconut and some sugar to taste (depending on how tart you like your raspberries).

Cook, stirring often until coconut absorbs most of the liquid-about 10 minutes. Spread over warm shortbread base.

Bake at 350 F for 10 minutes.

GREAT BIKING SNACKS

CHUNKY GRANOLA BARS

1 egg   2 tbsp. honey
½ cup peanut butter   2 cups granola

Combine egg, peanut butter and honey in a small saucepan. Cook over medium heat, stirring constantly, until mixture starts to bubble. Remove from heat, add granola and mix well.

Spread evenly in a greased 8 x 8-inch square pan. Chill until firm, cut into bars. Store in refrigerator.

GRANOLA GOODIES

1 orange, unpeeled
½ lb dried apricots
½ lb pitted dates

¼ cup granola
½ cup toasted sesame seeds, coconut
  or chopped nuts

Cut a thin slice from each end of an orange; cut orange into quarters and remove core. Put orange, apricots, dates and granola through the food grinder with the fine knife.

Mix well and put through grinder again. Mix again. Chill for one to two hours, until easy to handle. If mixture seems too liquid add wheat germ or meal replacement. Form fruit mixture into balls, about one inch in diameter; roll in sesame seeds, coconut or nuts.

Keep refrigerated.

Makes 36 pieces.

GRANOLA BARS

6 cups large rolled oats
1 cup each wheat germ, coconut
1 cup of nuts and seeds (assorted)
½ cup sesame seed
1 tsp. salt

1 ½ cup honey
¾ cup safflower oil
1 tbsp. vanilla
½ cup whole-wheat flour
2 eggs

In large bowl mix together the oats, wheat germ, coconut, nuts, seeds, salt, flour.

In a cooking pot mix and warm slightly the honey, oil and vanilla. Beat eggs and add to honey mixture. Pour over the dry ingredients and mix well. Spreads on a large oiled cookie sheet, and roll flat. Bake at 300 F for 40 minutes and cut into bars while still warm.

A SOUR NOTE

WITHOUT REFRIGERATION, milk soured quickly. Pioneer women learned to make cottage cheese by setting a pan of sour milk over a pot of hot water; the milk separated into curds and whey, which was strained through cheesecloth to squeeze out more whey. The remaining curds and whey were mixed with cream, butter, salt, and pepper, making a delicious addition to a pioneer dinner.

CHAPTER 3

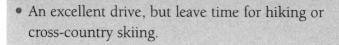

ROUTE 7: SANDHILL TO OWEN SOUND

- An excellent drive, but leave time for hiking or cross-country skiing.

Begin at the foot of Grey Road 40, near the Walters Falls sign, on Highway 26 just west of Georgian Peaks. Head southwest on Grey Road 4 for several miles.

As you cross over the old rail line at the start of Grey Road 40, picture the hill in front of you as much steeper, and sandy and dusty. Sandhill took its name from this hill.

Reliant on agriculture, the community of Sandhill is distinguished by those who settled here and the families they raised. Its first resident was a man named O'Grady who is listed as one of the earliest settlers in the entire Township of Collingwood. He received his land grant from the Crown in 1834.

Another of Sandhill's early settlers was Fred Marsh, who operated a creamery and apiary here. Marsh was the first butter-maker in the vicinity, and bees descendent from his apiary still make honey nearby.

Later residents of Sandhill distinguished themselves close to home and far away. J. J. Buchanan was Reeve of Collingwood Township from 1924 to 1929, and Marion Fields became a journalist and poet. Bella Goodfellow became a widely admired missionary who lived most of her adult life in India, and Cecil Dillon played in the National Hockey League for the New York Rangers.

Many of these fascinating people received their early education at the Sandhill School (Collingwood S.S. 14), built in 1874, which you'll find on the west side of the road at the top of the hill.

No one knows the age of the road you now travel. Grey Road 40, or the Walters Fall Road, was once a corduroy road. As you near the

Sandhill to Owen Sound

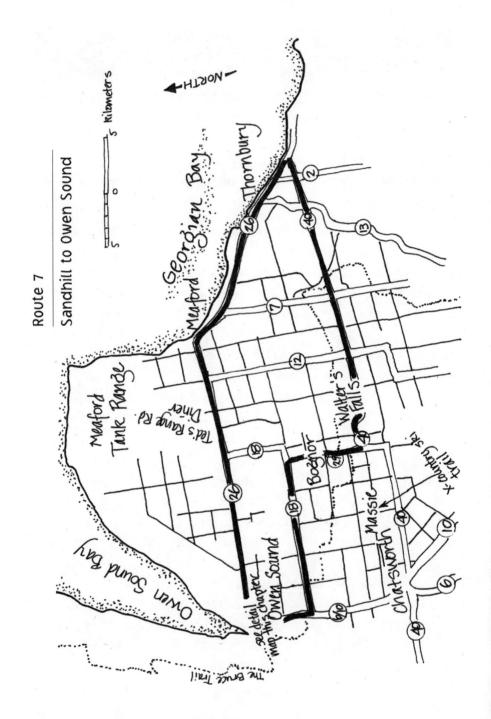

NORTH

Georgian Bay

Thornbury

Meaford

Meaford Tank Range

Owen Sound Bay

Owen Sound

Ted's Range Rd Diner

Walter's Falls

Bognor

Massie

Chatsworth

the country ski trail

See detail map this chapter

The Bruce Trail

Kilometers

72

village of Walters Falls, you'll notice that the land here is still terribly swampy. Corduroy roads, built of logs on top of swamps, made travel easier for settlers, but after a heavy rain or spring melt, the makeshift wooden roads shifted and sometimes even floated away.

Walters Falls was cut off from the rest of the world from December through April. In winter the road was buried under tons of snow that melted in the spring, creating a sea for settlers to travel after their long spell of isolation. Even today, the Walters Falls Road is continuously worked on and improved to keep it from shifting on the uneasy earth beneath it.

At the T past the forest, turn north (still on Grey Road 40) at the Walters Falls sign, round the bend, and at the next stop turn south (still on Grey Road 40) and into town.

Once the commercial centre of Holland, Euphrasia, St. Vincent and Sydenham Townships, Walters Falls is a confusing little village. All roads lead to Walters Falls . . . and once there, all sense of direction disappears. So many people have gotten lost here, the general store sells bumper stickers that read "We were lost in Walters Falls."

At the turn of the century, this little village was such an important place it received the Township's first telephone line from the Bell office in Meaford.

In the 1840s, Mr. John Walter, who harnessed the power of the nearby falls to run his sawmill, founded the settlement. Somewhere along the way, the place became known as Walters Falls.

As in most small communities, education was important to the people of Walters Falls. Their first school was in a shed behind the tavern. Soon, the school moved to the community hall, then to a small frame schoolhouse that was replaced by the current schoolhouse in 1889.

- **Great view and hiking.** Three sets of falls are located near Walters Falls. The prettiest can be found by turning west at the general store on what street and following the road to the falls at the old mill site.

At the general store, continue south and around the bend, follow the highway north. Continue to the next corner and follow Grey Road 18 west.

Before driving west on Grey Road 18, stop and get out of the car to look around. At the northeast corner of this isolated crossroads sits Union School Section 9, built in 1873. Its stone walls cracked, its back shed tired, the somewhat dishevelled landmark is showing its age.

The parents of the first children to attend U.S.S. 9 were obliged to supply the school with a quarter cord of chopped wood per student, delivered annually by March 1. When tenders were put out to have the wood supplied, parents simply paid a sum of twenty-five cents for each child to attend. With wood selling at forty-nine cents a cord, many parents paid far more for their children's education under this new system, but most thought it was worth it.

St. Paul's, the church across from the school, was built in 1890. Until then the school had served as a church. Residents of the Bognor and Walters Falls area still attend St. Paul's each Sunday.

Turn west at the schoolhouse intersection. Follow Grey Road 18 one last turn to the north and drive through Bognor, formerly Sydenham Mills. Drive straight, following the road west towards Owen Sound. Follow Grey Road 18 through the lights at Highways 6 and 10 until you reach the conservation area one-half kilometer ahead. Turn north on Grey Road 5 to Inglis Falls Conservation Area, well marked on the east side of the highway.

- **Great view, picnic, hiking, cross-country skiing.** When Peter Inglis saw the mighty Sydenham River roar and tumble over a craggy rockface into a gorge 59 feet below, he knew he had found his dream and his future.

Harnessing the powers of these waters, Inglis built his modest grist-mill below the falls that bear his name today. Settlers came from Sydenham (now Owen Sound), Mount Forest and from as far away as Collingwood, their oxen straining as they hauled the load to be ground into a season's flour and feed. He soon built a successful sawmill as well, a massive four-storey structure at the base of the falls.

Tragically, all that Peter Inglis worked for was swept away by fire in 1945, just eleven years after the Inglis family had sold the business. All that remain today are two millstones on display at the Conservation Area and bits of the mill's foundation.

What fire couldn't destroy were the beautiful waterfalls that drew Inglis to the edge of the Niagara Escarpment. They attract hundreds of sightseers annually.

Lord and Lady Dufferin were famous visitors here one summer in the late 1800s. The falls were a mere trickle then. A plan was hatched to hire a party of farmers to build a dam upstream from the falls along with a rudimentary set of floodgates to release the pent-up waters at just the right moment.

The day of the visit arrived and, as Lord and Lady Dufferin drew closer to their destination, a rider was dispatched to give a secret signal to the farmers. The honoured guests were just out of sight of the falls as the floodgates were released. The wall of water surged towards the gorge. As the visitors drew nearer, they could hear the rush, but still the falls were only a trickle. By the time Lord and Lady Dufferin arrived at their sightseeing destination, however, huge torrents of water were tumbling over the Escarpment and into the gorge below. The guests remarked at the beauty of this wonder of nature as their escorts tried to hurry them off before the secret was revealed.

Today, Inglis Falls lie within a 445-acre area protected by the Grey/Sauble Conservation Authority. Within its boundaries, the Sydenham River flows for 6 kilometers and plantlife, fish and mammals abound.

At the Conservation Area exit, turn north and follow the road to the Stop sign after the S-curve, turn south on Second Avenue to Harrison Park on the west side of the road.

- **Great hiking, biking, cross-country skiing, and picnics.** Lovely Harrison Park is situated on land the Harrison family sold to the city for the bargain price of $5,000 in 1912, at that time about half its true value. Aside from the trails for hiking, biking and skiing, the park has a miniature golf course, tennis courts, a playground, campsites, food facilities and washrooms.

Head north on Second Avenue to Owen Sound. For a quick return east, follow Highway 26 out of Owen Sound. (For a history of Highway 26, see Chapter 6, Collingwood to the Bruce Peninsula.)

The Ottawa nation who inhabited the Bruce Peninsula were members of the Algonkian-speaking group of Anishnabe, or kindred, nations, which includes the Ojibwa, the Mississauga, the Saulteaux and the Nipissing. The Algonkian were a northern people whose territories stretched from Labrador to the western plains, the south shores of Hudson Bay to the north shore of Lakes Superior and Huron and down into Georgian Bay.

Unlike the agricultural Petun, the Ottawa relied on hunting and gathering for their food supplies. During the winter months, they split up into small bands of extended families then spread out over a wide hunting area. The Ottawa were a spiritual people who relied on ritual, formalities and rites. Ceremonies were performed before the hunters searched for prey. Bears were clubbed in a particular way, their skulls kept for later ceremonies. No animal was ever killed for sport. Every bit of the animal was honoured in ceremony for providing food, clothing, sinew, oil and more.

Harrison Park / Inglis Falls - Owen Sound
By donation for trail fee.
There are 5 trails totalling 14 km.
60% are groomed and track set
twice a week. There are washrooms
and a restaurant. 20% easy, 40%
intermediate and 40% difficult.
Classic and telemark hill
Managed by: Grey /Sauble Conservation Authority
519-376-3076

Hibou, Sydenham Township
From Owen Sound drive north on 2nd Ave. E.
to East Bayshore Rd. Follow to Hibou
Conservation Area.
Fee by donation. There are 2 trails totalling
10 km. 100% easy - grooming possibly.
classic, wilderness trails.
managed by: Grey /Sauble Conservation
Authority / 519. 376. 3076

In summer, when the food supply was plentiful, the various nations congregated in large bands in good fishing areas. The Bruce Peninsula and southwest end of Georgian Bay near Owen Sound were perfect lands for the Ottawa. Berries and other plant foods, collected by the women, were plentiful. The men fished and hunted for wild game, more than satisfying the band's needs. Much of the summer food was smoked or dried, then stored for winter. If supplies ran short, the Ottawa knew they could rely on the Petun to the southeast, with whom they traded for corn.

The Ottawa were on the shores of Georgian Bay long before their lives were changed by the arrival of others. The European explorers of the 1600s brought diseases that devastated the native population and, at the same time, the Iroquois wars caused the dispersal of many Ottawa to Manitoulin Island. Others joined their Algonkian relatives, finding greater safety in numbers.

The Europeans were a curiosity to the Ottawa. In 1616, Samuel de Champlain had made his way into Georgian Bay and Lake Huron in the company of Etiènne Brûlé. But over two hundred years passed before English, Scottish and Irish pioneers settled the area. In the meantime, the Ojibwa, relatives of the Ottawa, settled here, calling their village Newash. Captain William Fitzwilliam Owen, who named the Sound for his brother, surveyed the waters. In 1856, the Village of Sydenham was officially named Owen Sound.

Shipping became the basis of this area's success. When the railway arrived in the 1880s, Owen Sound became a major centre of transport, the "Gateway to the West."

Ships here carried cargo from all over the world. A multitude of businesses, including many taverns and six breweries (only Toronto had more) opened throughout the town. All of this gave Owen Sound a reputation as a wild town. The United States opened a consulate, partially for its shipping concerns, but mainly to handle the cases of the drunken and imprisoned American sailors who needed bail before they missed their ships home.

In 1906, Owen Sound solved its problem. The town introduced prohibition, which lasted until 1972, making it the last dry city in Canada.

Despite this rowdiness, the people of Owen Sound quietly turned the city into a centre of commerce. And two young men from Owen Sound become Canadian heroes.

In the nearby village of Leith, a young artist named Tom Thomson was born. After apprenticing as a machinist at an Owen Sound company, Tom left the area in 1901, after which he developed a career as one of Canada's most distinguished painters. He was buried here after his mysterious death by drowning in Algonquin Park. Thomson's paintings of the near north inspired the Group of Seven.

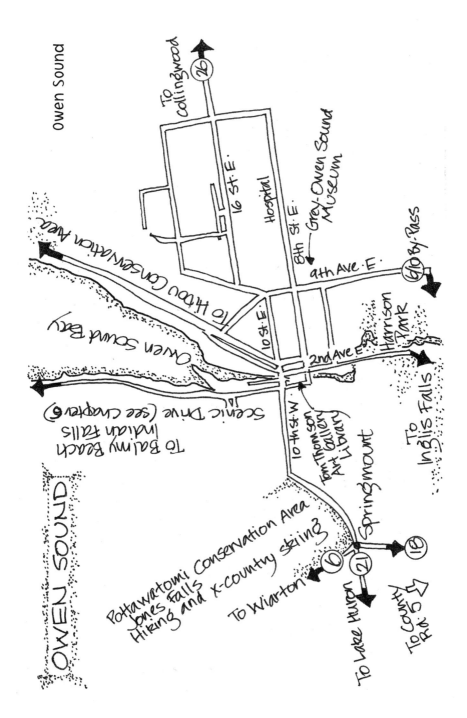

Owen Sound

OWEN SOUND

To Collingwood
26

16 St. E.

Hospital

8th St. E.

Grey-Owen Sound Museum

To Hibou Conservation Area

Owen Sound Bay

10 St. E.

4th Ave. E.

6/10 By-Pass

Harrison Park

2nd Ave. E.

To Inglis Falls

To Balmy Beach Indian Falls

Scenic Drive (see chapter 6)

10 1st W.

Tom Thomson Art Gallery Library

Springmount

To Wiarton

Pottawatomi Conservation Area
Jones Falls
Hiking and x-country skiing

6

21

18

To Lake Huron

To County Rd. 5

Billy Bishop was born in Owen Sound in 1894. At the age of seventeen, Billy left his home to enrol at the Royal Military College and three years later, in 1914, went to England with the 7th Canadian Mounted Rifles. By the end of the First World War, this brave young man was awarded the Victoria Cross, the Distinguished Service Order and the Military Cross (all simultaneously) as well as the Distinguished Flying Cross as Canada's most famous flying ace.

- **Farmer's Market.** Opened in 1850, the market is located behind City Hall in what was once the Water Works building, which itself dates from 1868.

- **The Billy Bishop Museum** is located in his childhood home at 948 Third Avenue West.

- **The Tom Thomson Gallery** includes paintings by Thomson and members of the Group of Seven. The gallery is located at 840 First Avenue West.

ROUTE 8: THE GEORGIAN TRAIL

- Good for hiking, biking, and cross-country skiing.

The Georgian Trail, built on a former train line, runs along the shoreline of the Bay following the path of Highway 26. It is marked on many of our maps including the Collingwood to Owen Sound map found in this chapter. We will follow this old rail line 32 kilometers from east to west, from Collingwood to Meaford.

Park your car at the Blue Mountain Mall just off Highway 26 in Collingwood. The trail begins near the grocery store. The route has many access points, but not all have parking. (See map on page 25.)

Georgian Trail - Collingwood to Meaford
I Trail - the old rail line between Collingwood and Meaford. Accessed at most intersections.
No grooming. Easy.
Total length: 32 kms.
Managed by: Georgian Cycle and Ski Trail Association c/o Georgian Triangle Tourist Ass. 705·445·7722·

Massie · Owen Sound ·
south on Massie Rd· cross I concession, climb a long hill, look for trail entrance on right. Trail map is on a bulletin board here.
No fee. There are 4 trails totalling 7 kms.
Classic· no grooming· 40% easy, 60% intermediate.

West Rocks· Owen Sound·
No fee, no grooming· There are 3 wilderness trails totalling 6 km·
In Owen Sound take 2nd Ave south east to County Rd· 5· Head west to 1st intersection; turn right and go north to end of road.
Small parking area on the right·

Pottawatomi Trails, Springmount
There is no fee and no grooming. There is I trail of 3 km. It is 100% easy and wilderness
Managed by: Grey / Sauble Conservation · Authority / 519·376·3076·

As you cycle the Georgian Trail, you'll want to take time to notice the natural wonders — a beaver dam built across a creek, or a deer gracefully moving through a maze of trees. You may catch the sweet smell of the apple blossoms or the strokes of red painted by the flight of the cardinal.

The beginnings of the Georgian Trail came from a conversation between Douglas Hall and Anne Bennett. Anne was then a Director with the Collingwood Chamber of Commerce. She brought Doug's idea of developing a cycle trail to Chamber, and it was there received with enthusiasm.

With help from Sheila Metras and the Georgian Triangle Tourist Association, the Trail committee cut through red tape, brought the municipalities and townships on board, arranged for rights-of-way through orchards and backyards, and raised thousands of dollars for the project. With the rails and ties removed, the rail bed graded and limestone screening laid, the Georgian Trail opened in October of 1989, a mere four years after the idea was hatched.

The story of the Georgian Trail wouldn't be complete without the history of Highway 26 and the rail line.

Starting in Midhurst and heading west, Highway 26 is one of the oldest roads in Georgian Baytripper. Now paved and well maintained, the road was carved from the wilderness to ease settlement of the southern shore of Georgian Bay.

One important historical figure in Grey County was Charles Rankin. A surveyor, he planned and supervised the laying out of vast areas of Southern Ontario. Rankin was born in Bytown (Ottawa) in the early 1800s and was brought to Collingwood and St. Vincent Townships, then called Alta and Zero, in 1833.

The government rewarded military and naval personnel and United Empire Loyalists with Crown grants of lands. In 1834, Rankin and his teams of locally hired men recognized the need for roads and suggested to the Commissioner of Crown Land that Rankin survey a route from the Sunnidale Region to the mouth of the Bighead River (now Meaford) for a cost of 320 pounds. Rankin oversaw, through contractors and subcontractors, the cutting of what they called the Lakeshore Road. Throughout the 1830s, the Lakeshore Road competed with the Old Mail Road to the south as the main road into the townships.

Stumps and rocks reigned supreme on the Lakeshore Road, and during the wet times of the year, it was impassable. When travel was possible, blazes cut into the trees indicated the path. However, settlers along the route used the same system to mark the trails into their homesteads. It wasn't uncommon to hear travellers shouting for help in the middle of the wilderness, totally lost and confused. Stories tell of pioneer families guiding the field hands in with bells, horns and gunshots.

In 1855, when the rail line came to Collingwood, the Lakeshore Road became the most-used route to the west. With the increase in travellers, the road was improved until it slowly became a major highway.

That rail line changed more than just the Lakeshore Road. The Toronto, Simcoe and Lake Huron Railway Co. came to Hens and Chickens (named after the offshore rocks in Collingwood Harbour). This was the first of the Ontario "long lines." From Hens and Chickens, goods and passengers were sent on to Sault Sainte Marie, Chicago or Owen Sound by ship, and to nearer destinations by horse and wagon on the Lakeshore Road.

The settlements of Thornbury and Meaford grew. By 1871, the North Grey Railway constructed the Collingwood to Owen Sound line, the roadbed on which you now cycle. As with the Georgian Trail, the rail line was financed by both the province and the townships. And as with the Trail, disputes arose as to just whose land this rail line would pass over. Construction was halted at Thornbury for a full year due to one such dispute, but the line finally moved on, reaching Meaford in late 1872.

This line saw many changes in ownership over a few short years. First, the North Grey Railway Company amalgamated with the Toronto, and Muskoka Junction Railway Company (previously amal-

gamated with the Toronto, Simcoe, Lake Huron Railway Company), to become the Northern Extension Railway Company. In 1887, the Grand Trunk Railway took ownership of the line and, some forty years later, it amalgamated with the Canadian National Railway.

Unbelievably, the line was originally laid with a wider gauge than the Toronto to Collingwood line. This necessitated off-loading and reloading all goods and passengers at Collingwood. The mammoth and expensive job of ripping up and relaying the track in standard gauge started in 1881, ten years after the original line was started.

Let's ride the rails now, from Collingwood to Meaford through Craigleith. First stop, Craigleith.

During the winter months of the 1940s and 1950s, this station was busy. A ski train called the Weekend Special carried a hundred or more passengers singing and laughing all the way from Toronto to Craigleith. Stories of those trips are chuckled over by some of those same passengers today.

One skier showing others how to repair skis started a fire that burned through the baggage car. There was the New Year's Eve Special that stopped in Barrie for a moccasin dance on the ice, then carried on to Craigleith. On stormy nights, drivers picked passengers up at the Craigleith Depot, cramming as many as possible into their cars or horse-drawn sleighs, then hoped they'd make it up the steep hill to Blue Mountain.

In better weather, few paid the 25 cents for a ride, but some climbed onto the sleigh, huddled under the buffalo robe, and arrived at Blue in style. The rest trudged up the steep hill on Winter Park Road (now Blue Mountain Road), skis weighing down one shoulder, boots slung over the other, poles assisting with the climb.

The pioneering days of skiing changed with the increased use of the automobile. Fewer people used the ski train, and it ceased operation in the early 1960s. The Craigleith Depot still stands, however.

More than a reminder of the Weekend Special and ski days past, this much-anticipated rail line made its rapid advance towards Craigleith in 1871. Gangs of men laboured long hours. The sound of sledgehammers striking iron rang out across the county. The coming of the rail meant a new way of life for residents.

With a train twice a day in each direction, a trip into Collingwood for supplies could be completed in a few hours. High school students, who once boarded in Collingwood, could commute and stay home with their families.

A year after the line came through Craigleith, on land donated by Alexander Fleming (Sir Sandford Fleming's father), the Craigleith station was built. Designed in the fashion of the day, the station had separate waiting rooms for men and women, the baggage area, stationmaster's quarters, and a ticket window.

The Craigleith Depot is an important piece of our heritage, the only remaining station built along this "long line." In May the Depot is splendid when hundreds of lilac bushes east of the site are fragrant with blossom. Lilacs grow annually in adverse conditions. Lilac bushes, a hearty symbol of the settlers' endurance, mark abandoned farmhouses throughout Southern Ontario. They were planted by the families that once lived there. The Craigleith lilacs were said to be planted by Alexander and Sir Sandford Fleming.

- **Don't miss the Sheffield Park Black History Museum.** As you pass Osler Bluffs Road east of Craigleith, cross the highway and go north on the Osler Road to a museum that celebrates the heritage of Ontario's black citizens. Admission is modest and the Sheffield family or their many volunteers will gladly show you around.

One cabinet displays the medals and trophies of track star Raymond Lewis, who was born in Collingwood. Mr. Lewis competed in the 1932 Olympics, where he ran against Jesse Owens and won a bronze medal.

The museum has many wooden ship models handmade by Eddie Sheffield. These replicas include a slave ship and models of Great Lakes ships where many blacks worked and earned the "freedom gained by being on the water." One chilling display is a set of slave chains. The huge brass manacles bear the tag Jeremiah Baird, Slave Auction.

The collection also includes many photographs of black settlers who came to Grey and Bruce Counties via the Underground Railway or as United Empire Loyalists.

 • **Great view and picnic.** For a picnic with a great view and the scent of lilacs, park near the Craigleith Community Centre, a former schoolhouse behind the Depot.

Craigleith Provincial Park and Oil Shale Works

In the late 1850s, a Collingwood lawyer named Colonel Pollard experimented with the shale found along Georgian Bay's shoreline near Craigleith. He discovered that extreme heat separated fossil fuels from shale. The shale was extracted from a field south of the present-day highway, just east of Arrowhead Road, and was then heated in ovens — which caused numerous fires there. Unfortunately, with the discovery of petroleum pools near Petrolia, expensive shale oil was less in demand and the Shale Oil Works ceased operating in 1861, after only two years. All that remains is a plaque in Craigleith Provincial Park.

Next stop, Camperdown.

The locomotives were powerful, pulling cars packed with goods and passengers over hundreds of miles, but a low-grade hill, not to mention snowdrifts, slowed them down to a crawl. The railroaders of the late 1800s hadn't invented an efficient way to push snow aside. Male passengers were warned that they might have to dig and push.

Even with this manpower, many a train became snowbound, sometimes for days. Women and children tried to stay warm and sane while rail workers, male passengers and men from nearby settlements dug out the train. Finally, someone invented the snowplow.

Old photos show corridors, walls up to ten feet high, cleared by these plows. These corridors were sometimes used for walking. Unfortunately, trains often struck livestock and people alike because they couldn't escape over the walls of snow.

 • **Great view and picnic.** Just before you reach Camperdown and Georgian Peaks, you'll cross Ward's Road and discover a great shale beach for a picnic, a swim, a view of the water, or fossil hunting. The shale pieces on this beach contain seashells, seaweed, and trilobites, marine life of 445 million years ago.

As you ride past the Peaks and towards Camperdown Road, imagine this stretch in the late 1800s. The Peaks was the site of a three-storey hotel and resort called the Wensley House. Across the way at Delphi Point was a successful sanitarium. Both resorts took advantage of the new rail line, a nearby sulphur spring and the Bay itself to attract clientele.

In the 1860s, goods rumbled along the upgraded Lakeshore Road, then called the Gravel Road. Up to thirty teams of horses arrived at once. Horses and men needed food, drink and an overnight rest. Two innkeepers, Misters Spies and Milligan, opened inns, side by side, on the southeast corner of the Gravel and Camperdown Roads. But the coming of the railway to Owen Sound within twenty years ended the era of the great wagon teams and the need for inns.

 • **In the fall, look for roadside apple stands along Highway 26.**

Next stop, Thornbury.

It took only five months for the new rail line to reach Thornbury. It was a momentous occurrence in this tiny community. Thornbury expected an increase of new residents and visitors and prosperity. The spectacle of the line brought excitement to the town.

The workers of the Toronto Construction Company likely attracted their largest audience while constructing the wooden bridge across the Beaver River. Because sparks from the coal-burning steam engines caused fires, three-foot-square platforms were built at each end of the bridge to hold filled water barrels. Children used to play on the bridge. There by dare or accident, with the trains bearing down on them, they would crouch, eyes wide, knuckles white, beside the barrels as screeching iron, smoke, wind, and whistle roared past them.

The final passenger train left Thornbury in July 1960, and twenty years later, the last freight train ended the town's railway era.

- **Picnic spot.** As you cross over Grey Road 40 to the west of the Peaks, look for Council Beach on the east side of the road off Highway 26. One of the few sandy beaches along this section of shoreline, it's a great place for a picnic and swim.

- **Picnic spot.** Don't forget beautiful Thornbury Harbour. Sit on the grass or on the rocks by the water, and watch the gorgeous sailboats come and go.

Last stop, Meaford.

The Toronto Construction Company finally brought the railway to Meaford in 1872. But they brought more than rails and ties. Apparently southern Georgian Bay was never home to poison ivy until the coming of the train. Mixed in with the earth that lined the rail bed were the roots and seeds of that irritating weed. Residents of Meaford were soon scratching a mysterious rash that spread to other towns and villages along the line. Poison ivy had found a new home.

The Hunters' Special was a weekend train that ran each fall in the early 1900s. The Special let deer hunters disembark at any station between Collingwood and Owen Sound. As wooded lands disappeared because of lumbering and farming, hunting declined, and so, the Hunters' Special, like all other trains along the line, ceased operation.

- **Great view and picnic.** Halfway between Thornbury and Meaford you'll cross over the Christie Beach Road. Down the hill is a large, sandy beach with washroom facilities and a great view of the bay.

Collingwood to Meaford: The Schoolhouse Journey

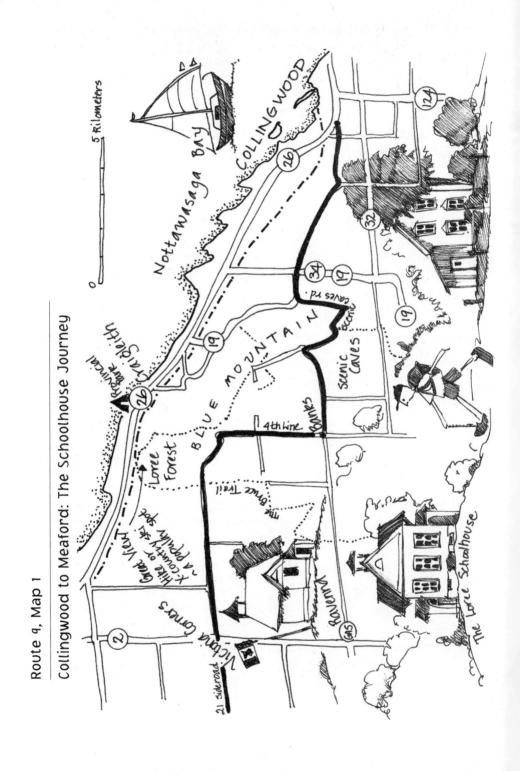

ROUTE 9: COLLINGWOOD TO MEAFORD: THE SCHOOLHOUSE JOURNEY

- Good for car, mountain biking, cross-country skiing, hiking.

Begin on the Blue Mountain Road west of Collingwood. Past the Osler Bluffs Road, as you near Blue Mountain Resort, turn south onto Sideroad 15-16 to the Scenic Caves.

During the mid-1800s, when Grey County became settled, the families around Rob Roy, Duncan and Banks travelled to Collingwood once a year for supplies. They wanted the easiest, fastest trail over that formidable obstacle, "the Blue Hills." The road you follow, Sideroad 15-16, was one of those trails.

As you climb 700 vertical feet of switchbacks to the top, keep in mind this road was first used by horses pulling wagons.

- **Historic site.** As you near the turn onto Sideroad 15-16, look along the tops of the hills for a prominent rock jutting out from the Escarpment just south of Blue Mountain Resorts. This is Ekarenniondi, sacred to many nations who came hundreds of miles to show respect. The Petun, Huron, Ottawa and Ojibwa believe this rock is a living entity that guards the path to the afterlife.

  In the Petun, Huron and Ottawa traditions, this rock contains the spirit Oscotarah, or Pierce-head. As the soul of a dead person passes through Ekarenniondi, always from west to east, Oscotarah mercifully draws the brain through a hole he has pierced in the skull, thus relieving the soul of any human memory and making the transition to the new state a happy one.

  Similarly, the Ojibwa believe the soul passes through Ekarenniondi from west to east. The Ojibwa believe spirits, known as "the little people," live in the fissures of this sacred rock, to ease the passage of souls into the next life.

The Huron, Petun and Ojibwa nations mourned and celebrated the passing of their relatives and friends with a Feast of the Dead. The Ojibwa held the feast every summer when the tribes gathered for fishing and food gathering. Up to 1,500 people might gather for this important feast. The Petun and Huron celebrated the Feast of the Dead when they moved their villages every ten to twelve years. After taking down the villages, the remains of loved ones were brought together and buried with totems, sentimental belongings and pelts in a huge pit. One such burial pit was discovered near the Osler Bluff Road during construction.

Ekarenniondi was the site of an International Council of Indian Nations meeting some 300 years ago to discuss means of driving the French from the area.

The Scenic Caves
At the top, you'll find the Scenic Caves on the south side of Sideroad 15-16. Over millions of years, this cool, damp maze was carved out of the limestone by ice and water. Collingwood resident Alfred Staples saw the potential of the caves as a tourist attraction and purchased the land for just $750 in 1934. Mr. Staples walked from Collingwood to the Caves each Saturday and Sunday to sell tickets and guide visitors on the tour. He launched one of the most popular tourist destinations in the Georgian Triangle, attracting some 50,000 visitors annually.

- **Great view.** Past the scenic caves, continue on Sideroad 15-16, around the S-turn to the top of the hill to the second bend for a panoramic view of Collingwood, the Bay and the cliffs of the Escarpment. This is a great site for fall colour viewing.

Continue along Sideroad 15-16 to the Stop sign and turn north on the 4th Concession to Banks.

In 1876, William Johnson named his new postal station Banks after a town in England, although locals joke it was named after the huge snowbanks that pile up each winter. The village thrived on farming and farming and lumber; three sawmills operated here at one time.

A skating rink was built at these crossroads on ice made from pure spring water. Residents skated and played hockey here into the 1900s. What a wonderful sight to see horses and cutters tied in a row, the long blades of skaters flashing in the moonlight.

Turn north at Banks on the 4th Concession, which turns into Sideroad 21/22. Follow the three sweeping curves that take you to Loree.

On the north side of Sideroad 21/22, you'll come to School Section 7. At one point, the school shut down for lack of students. Luckily, however, a large pioneer family brought enough children to warrant its reopening. In June 1937 the schoolhouse was struck by lightning and burned to the ground. Much to the chagrin of the students sitting exams, they were simply moved to Orange Hall across the road. The new school opened in November 1937. This schoolhouse, now a private residence, still has the school bell in the tower and chalkboards on some of the walls — and it too has been struck by lightening.

- **For great mountain biking and cross-country skiing,** find the dirt road on the north side of Sideroad 21/22, just west of the final bend into Loree (across from the two-storey house near the bend).

  The Loree Forest Loop is a flat, easy, enjoyable tour for almost anyone and is especially good for the beginner mountain biker, summer hiker, and cross-country skier. The students and teachers of Georgian Bay Secondary School cut a cross-country loop in the early 1970s.

To find the Loop, follow the dirt road up the steep hill into the forest. Past the crown of the hill, look for a small marker, or just look for the beaten path. Stay right at all forks.

Loree sits on the brow of the Niagara Escarpment, where there is scant protection from the famous winds that come howling across the Bay and straight into the settlement, bringing rain, lightning strikes, snow and mayhem. In winter, travellers face whiteouts and snowdrifts.

What possessed the Loree brothers, John, William and George, to settle here in the 1870s? Like many pioneers, the brothers were likely ignorant of Ontario's severe winters. By 1878, all the Lorees had left the area, leaving only their name and a few stray apple trees.

You'll come across a present-day farmer's field, in the middle of the forest, on your way to the top of Georgian Peaks.

 • **Great view and picnic spot.** The view from the top of the Peaks is spectacular. The Bay seems huger from this vantage point than from anywhere else — Thornbury tucked in below at the shore, Christian Island in the distance — and from here you can see how this once-pristine wilderness has been changed by fire, the lumber trade, farming and the ski industry.

Back on the pavement, past the Loree Schoolhouse, Sideroad 21/22 descends to Grey Road 2 and Victoria Corners.

Assuring their children of some form of education was of utmost importance to early settlers. One of the first establishments in most settlements was a school, whether it be classes held in someone's home with members of the community acting as teachers or with a hired teacher in a schoolhouse built for the purpose.

Until 1864, the children of Loree, Victoria, Sandhill and Camperdown all attended the same school. By 1910, there were enough students living near Victoria to warrant the building of

Collingwood to Meaford: The Schoolhouse Journey

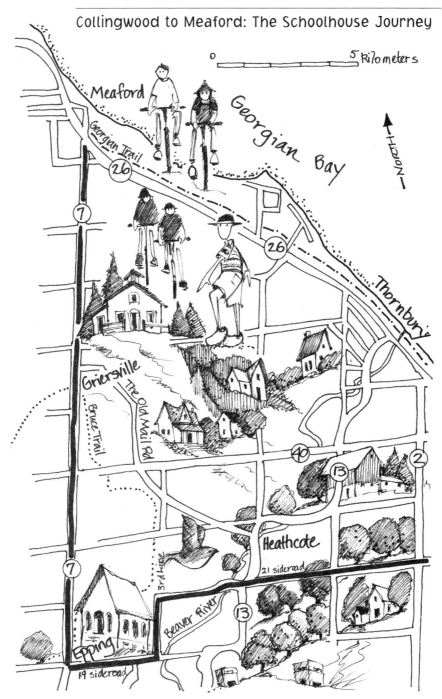

School Section 17 at the northeast corner of the Victoria Corners crossroads. A private residence today, this building was a school until 1968.

- **Great view and picnic spot.** Two Stop signs past Victoria Corners, cross over Grey Road 13 below Heathcote, and you'll take a country bridge over the wide and lazy Beaver River. The road narrows and fields and trees envelop you in a sea of green along one of the prettiest drives in *Georgian Baytripper.*

- **Canoe access off the 19th Sideroad, one line south.**

Continue past the Stop sign at Grey Road 2 onto the 3rd Line. After negotiating some tight bends, and passing Kimbercote Farm, look for the tiny schoolhouse on the west side of the 3rd Line.

Euphrasia School Section 21 proves the determination of our pioneers to educate their children. During the 1890s, having lost in a long struggle with the government to be named a school section, the people of Quiet Valley started their own school in a family home. This convinced the Township Council that a school was necessary and well-deserved. Built in 1900, Euphrasia S.S. 21 was home school to generations of local children until it closed in 1967.

Turn west at the Stop sign from 3rd Line to Sideroad 19. At the next Stop, turn north onto Grey Road 7, also called the Eric Winkler Parkway.

The final two schoolhouses on our Schoolhouse Journey are found along this road. They are also the oldest.

When these building opened, a day at school was as simple as the one-room structure itself. You would find your desk and seat yourself among the other children nearest your age. Your classmates might be as young as five, but some could be as old as eighteen. Many of the older boys skipped classes from spring till snowfall because, though completing grade eight was an important goal, they were needed to work their families' farms and fields.

Class began and the schoolroom hushed. The little room, smoky from the wood fire in the corner, held all eight grades. One teacher mustered all her skill and knowledge to keep everybody in the room interested and quiet.

Your teacher might board with a family, or a community sometimes built living quarters at the schoolhouse. In the 1860s, teachers earned about $100 per year. By 1880, they earned $250 a year, and by 1900, they earned nearly $500 per annum.

To maintain and heat the school, parents were charged 25 cents per year for each student. Some parents bartered; in March, they delivered a cord of wood for every two pupils attending.

The school day's structure remained the same for a century. School began at 9 o'clock with dinner from noon to 1, then classes again until 4, with two recesses in between. For much of the day not a sound was heard from anyone but the teacher. Sports and school trips? Not in these schools. The Three Rs and discipline were the focus. At 4 o'clock, pupils left the schoolhouse single file, raced home to do chores, played, and prepared for the next day.

Modern-day visitors in search of schoolhouses will next come upon Euphrasia School Section 6, built in 1875 and the first school in the township. Called the Fairmont School, it was named after Fair Mountain.

Descending the hill further, you come into the hamlet of Griersville. Here stands the final schoolhouse of our journey, School Section 14, built in 1853, on the west side of the junction of Highway 7 and the Old Mail Road.

Griersville was named after Andrew Grier, the Superintendent for the Schools of Grey County during the 1860s, and School Inspector for Collingwood Township from 1871 to 1896. A century ago, only one log school opposite the present school served Griersville, Fairmont and Quiet Valley.

MEAFORD OPERA HOUSE

Follow the Eric Winkler Parkway towards the water. At the lights on Highway 26, turn west to Meaford.

If an artist painted a picture of the quintessential Ontario town, it would be Meaford. The view from the east is one of the prettiest on Georgian Bay. First impressions are of the tower of the United church standing tall among the trees and, looming in the background, the massive wall of the Dobie building. With the descent into town, however, you'll notice side streets crowded with trees, classic homes trimmed in gingerbread and white paint, and a downtown that seems untouched by time.

Meaford began as a 2,000-acre parcel of cedar and brushwood surveyed by Charles Rankin. Early settlers arrived in flat bateaux. They came up the Bighead River to Peggy's Landing, named for the wife of David Miller, an Irish settler. The Millers came early to St. Vincent Township, and built the first mill on the Bighead, where they ground flour and meal.

Another early settler, William Stephenson, knew the importance of food, drink and rest. He opened the Georgian Inn near the shoreline in the early 1840s. The combined hotel, tavern and the first post office had a small wharf where boats docked for the night.

Meaford was named by surveyor William Gibbard for the county seat of Sir John Jervis, the Earl of St. Vincent. Its nickname was "The Golden Town" because of the sunrises and sunsets reflected on the nearby waters.

History remains alive in this town's streets, which are named after such British Navy admirals as Collingwood, Trowbridge, Nelson and Sykes. Meaford also boasts a distinctive architectural heritage in the large number of turn-of-the-century buildings.

One such building is the Town Hall Opera House. Built in 1908 as a monument to the prosperity of Meaford, it serves the same function today as then: town office, courthouse, police station (until 1998), and a place for people to congregate. The hall's sweeping staircases, tall Doric columns and oblong windows recall a Georgian manor. The walls of the performance hall echo with voices from the past; Jiggs and Maggie Blackstone, John Diefenbaker and Lester Pearson all appeared here.

Meaford has faced hardship and disaster. Several times, the Bighead River flooded its banks. Fire has destroyed several heritage properties. Yet through all of this, Meaford's residents have worked together, remaining easygoing and friendly, as befits a quintessential Ontario town.

- **Great view.** Mount Hope Methodist Church, at the corner of Sideroad 19 and Grey Road 7, was built in 1887 for the people of Epping, one of the earliest settlements in Euphrasia Township. Today Epping is best known for the Beaver Valley and the Kimberley Bluffs Lookout. This is also a great place from which to view the fall colours.

The Temple Hill Loop

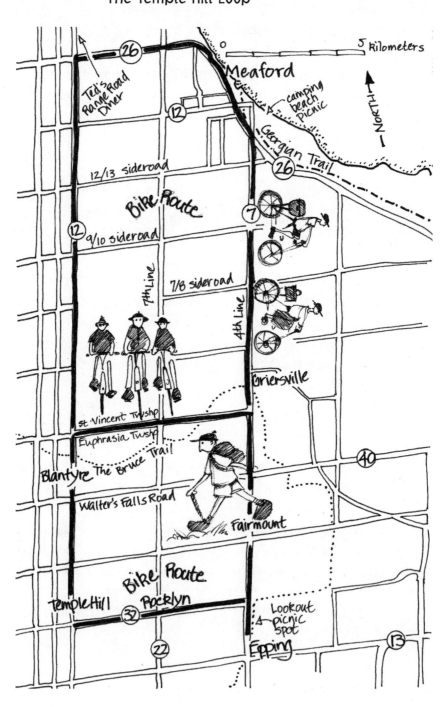

ROUTE 10: THE TEMPLE HILL LOOP

- Good for cars and mountain bikes.

Start this 24.5-kilometer journey on the east side of the highway at the Epping Lookout on the Eric Winkler Parkway. Follow Grey Road 7 north to Grey Road 32, where you will turn west to Rocklyn.

Rocklyn has been called many names since 1847. First came the Blacks of County Armagh, Ireland, who crossed miles of ocean and wilderness to settle at Black's Corners. Within a few years, the entrepreneurial Martin family opened a store and a hostel not far from the Blacks. Soon the crossroads at what is now the intersection of County Roads 22 and 32 was called Martin's Corners. During the 1860s, the Maines purchased the Martins' businesses; Maine's Corners became the name of the settlement. The Dyers bought the store and hostel in 1870. You can easily guess at the new name. The residents of the settlement soon began to call it Shornhagen, avoiding anyone's "Corners" entirely. And then when the post office opened in 1875, the name Rocklyn stuck.

One of the most interesting buildings in Grey County occupies the southeast corner. The original Lorne Hotel, named for the Marquis of Lorne, then governor general of Canada, was built in 1880 by W. H. Dodson. An impressive building, it contained thirteen guest bedrooms, a dining room with seating for one hundred, a bar-

room (gentlemen only), an upstairs sitting room (ladies only), a post office, a store and quarters for the Dodson family. Opened during a busy period in Rocklyn's history, the Lorne hosted hundreds of travellers, comfortably and safely, until July 12, 1891.

A warm midsummer's thunderstorm became a disaster that night when the hotel was struck by lightening. Flames quickly engulfed the frame building and it soon burned to the ground. Fortunately, everyone escaped the blaze. W. H. Dodson would not let his business be destroyed, though, and with the help of friends and neighbours, he bought materials and rebuilt the Lorne Hotel exactly like the original.

Later, Dodson sold the Lorne to the Curry family, who maintained the business into the 1920s. The last remaining Curry was Miss Barbara Curry, a schoolteacher who lived in the family quarters until her death in 1979. Miss Curry closed the hotel but continued to live there, with each room with still furnished as when it was a hotel. Following Miss Curry's death, many area residents had their first glimpse of this grand old hotel's interior at an estate auction. Today, the Lorne Hotel sits vacant, a fascinating relic of Rocklyn's past.

Continue west on Grey Road 32 from Rocklyn, past the Stop sign and onto the dirt road to Grey Road 12. Turn north onto Grey Road 12.

In the early years of Canadian settlement, religion was crucial to a pioneer's life. In nearly all communities, the first gatherings were for Bible readings and religious services. In many senses, Temple Hill Village is Temple Hill the church.

Robert Breadner, an early settler from County Armagh, Ireland, was a devout man. Mr. Breadner held church services in his log cabin beginning in 1858. Families would walk as far as six miles through the bush to attend. Recognizing the need for a proper place of worship, Mr. Breadner donated the land for the community's first church.

That original modest log structure was built where the cemetery is today. In honour of their benefactor, the congregation named their church the Temple for the Presbyterian church Breadner attended in Ireland. Upon his death, Robert Breadner was the first person buried in the Temple Hill Cemetery.

In 1880, Reverend James Fraser McLaren was called on to preside over the Temple Hill and Knox Holland Churches. His permanency warranted the building of a manse. This enormous brick home overwhelmed the little log church. The manse, now a private home, can be seen on the corner by the cemetery.

With worshippers coming from miles around, the congregation grew rapidly. A larger brick church at Temple Hill was built in 1887 on land purchased from Mr. James Boyd. The settlers donated many building materials and much labour. Today, the Temple Hill Church is one of the few rural churches still holding services regularly. Its congregation owes a great deal to those faithful pioneers of the 1800s who built this church, figuratively and literally.

Like so many isolated Ontario settlements in the 19th century, Temple Hill had no doctor. Home remedies often came to the rescue. Appendicitis or a broken limb put the sufferer in grave danger, while cholera or dysentery was usually fatal.

Often, a family member was sent on an epic journey to fetch a doctor. During the winter months, a 5-kilometer hike might as well be 500 kilometers. The messenger could get lost in a confusing maze of trails. Too often people died simply because they were too far from help.

The dead were buried in simple pine caskets built by a family member. Because stones were expensive, graves were marked with a wooden cross. There is the story of a pioneer woman from Temple Hill who was distraught over the loss of her husband. Determined to honour his memory with an inscribed gravestone, she spent hour after hour churning butter, then walked the 20 kilometers to Meaford in the vague hope of selling her wares, or trading it for the stone and carving. Sadly, this tale has no names or ending.

We believe one of the worn headstones in the graveyard at Temple Hill is the memorial to that man and his loving wife.

 • **Great view.** As you continue north on Grey Road 12, you will pass through Blantyre with a lovely view of the Bay and the surrounding lands.

Blantyre, or "Warm Retreat," was closely related to Temple Hill during the late 1800s. Only 4 kilometers apart, they shared the Temple Hill Church, the doctor in Blantyre, and Euphrasia School Section 12.

Built in Blantyre, the school sat on land leased from Mr. James Stitt at a price of one cent per year, payable on the first of each May. The ninety-nine-year lease came with a stipulation. If at any point the school closed for a period of six consecutive months or more, the land would revert back to Stitt's farm. Euphrasia S.S. 12 finally closed in 1968.

The Blantyre community used to be large enough to support a grist mill, a general store and post office with five employees, and two highly accomplished weavers who made beautiful soft flannels. But the industrial revolution and the mechanical mills of Meaford put the village's weavers out of business. The old-style grist mill hung on into the 1920s but eventually closed. The general store stayed in business until 1972. Unfortunately, the building was destroyed by fire in 1988. Only the Blantyre Community Centre, just north of the settlement on the east side of the road, remains as a lasting reminder of this village's heyday.

To conclude this journey, drive along Grey Road 12 through the countryside north of Blantyre. Turn east on the St. Vincent–Euphrasia Townline. Follow this to the T at Grey Road 7, where you can turn south, and return to Epping for a fabulous picnic at the Lookout.

RECIPES

WILD RICE STUFFED TROUT

½ cup water
1 tbsp. butter
¼ cup wild rice
2 tbsp. chopped onion
¾ cup chopped fresh spinach greens

¾ cup sliced mushrooms
1 clove garlic, minced
¼ tsp. dried basil
1–2 lb trout

In a small saucepan, bring water and 1 tbsp. butter to a boil. Add wild rice, cover and simmer 30 minutes. In a small skillet prepare vegetables on medium heat. Melt 1 tbsp. of the butter and add vegetables, garlic and basil, sauté until all moisture evaporates (3–4 minutes.)

Remove from heat and stir in cooked, drained rice. Wipe inside cavity of fish with paper towels. Stuff cavity with rice mixture and place in a foil-lined baking dish. Melt the remaining 1 tbsp. butter and pour over fish. Bake uncovered at 450 F allowing 10–12 minutes per inch of stuffed thickness.

BROCCOLI SOUP

1 large bunch of broccoli
2 or 3 medium potatoes, cubed
1 onion
1 tbsp. oil

1 tbsp. flour
2 cups of stock
Salt and pepper
Cinnamon

Cut broccoli into pieces and skin stalk. Steam until tender. Puree broccoli with water used for steaming.

Sauté onion in oil until transparent; add potatoes. Stir in flour to just cover onion and potatoes. Add stock, salt and pepper. Cook, stirring occasionally until potatoes are cooked. Puree in blender.

In a saucepan add potato and broccoli mixture; add more stock if needed. Simmer for 5–10 minutes. Serve with a sprinkling of cinnamon.

QUICK VEGGIE BREAD

½ cup chopped spinach leaves
½ cup grated carrot
1 scallion
2 ⅓ cups flour
4 tbsp. grated Parmesan cheese
2 tbsp. honey, slightly warmed
2 tbsp. baking powder

¾ tsp. salt
¾ tsp. dried thyme
⅛ tsp. nutmeg
1 cup milk
¼ cup oil
1 egg

Preheat oven to 325 F.

Butter a loaf pan. Chop the spinach, grate the carrot, and chop the scallion. In a large bowl, combine flour, 2 tbsp. Parmesan, baking powder, salt thyme and nutmeg.

In a separate bowl, combine the milk, oil, honey and egg. Stir the milk mixture and chopped vegetables into the flour mixture until all ingredients are just moistened. Spoon batter into the prepared pan. Sprinkle with the remaining 2 tbsp. Parmesan.

Bake until a toothpick stuck into the center comes clean, 50–60 minutes. Cool 10 minutes. Remove from the pan and cool completely before slicing.

OATMEAL BUTTER TART SQUARES

CRUST
½ cup butter
⅛ cup sugar

1 cup flour
Pinch salt

Crumble together. Press into 9 x 9-inch pan. Bake at 350 F for 5–10 minutes or until lightly browned.

TOP
¾ cup honey
2 eggs, beaten
¾ cups each of quick cooking oats,
   coconut and packed brown sugar

½ cups each butter or margarine,
   currants and chopped walnuts

Combine all ingredients and mix well. Pour onto crust. Bake at 350 F, 40–45 minutes or until filling browns and knife blade inserted near centre comes out clean. Cut into squares.

A Quick Salad

1 ½ cups romaine lettuce
1 ½ cups fresh spinach, hard stems
    removed
½ cup sliced fresh mushrooms
¼ cup sliced red onion
8 cherry tomatoes
¼ cup sliced red or green pepper
¼ cup grated carrot

DRESSING
3 tbsp. vinegar
6 tbsp. safflower oil
1 garlic, minced
½ tsp. mustard powder
½ tsp. dried dill

Put all ingredients in a small jar and shake vigorously. Toss dressing into salad when ready to serve.

Moist Pumpkin Bread

3 ½ cups all purpose flour
2 tsp. baking powder
½ tsp. baking soda
1 ½ tsp. salt (opt.)
1 tsp. cinnamon
½ tsp. ground cloves
4 lightly beaten eggs

1 ¾ cups honey
2 cups mashed pumpkin
⅔ cup water
½ cup oil
⅔ cup chopped walnuts
⅔ cup raisins

Sift first 6 ingredients. Beat eggs, oil, honey, pumpkin and water. Make a well in the centre of dry ingredients and add liquid ingredients, one cup at a time. Mix only enough to moisten. Mix in walnuts and raisins. Pour into two greased 9 x 5-inch loaf pans and bake 1 hour at 325 F.

Wrap and store 24 hours before serving. This loaf freezes well.

Red and Black Salad

1 cup whole pitted ripe California
    olives
2 cups cherry tomatoes, halved
½ lb small fresh mushrooms, sliced
    (about 2 cups)
½ cup olive oil

3 tbsp. chopped fresh basil
    (1 ½ tbsp. dried)
2 cloves garlic, minced
3 tbsp. Parmesan cheese
1–2 cups torn spinach or lettuce

Combine olives, tomatoes and mushrooms and greens in a bowl. Combine the remaining ingredients in a jar, shake and pour over salad. Toss well.

Eat sage for a long life and "glowing" health.

Soak anise seeds in alcohol and drink in small quantities for a digestive aid.

Drink chamomile to help "frail humanity in distress."

Gargle hyssop in boiled water for sore throat.

Take catnip for insomnia. (Valerian, the active ingredient, is used today as a tranquillizer.)

Eat cicely, a kind of parsley, for flu and headaches.

Take foxglove for ulcers and dropsy. (The plant is the source of digitoxin, used in the care of heart disease.)

Use monkshood as a sedative or painkiller. (Warning: it is a poisonous plant.)

Eat the blue flowers of the borage plant for courage and joy.

To cure sores, rashes, boils, and swelling, use a poultice of steeped leaves, sot stems, and flowers, of musk mallow, a cousin to the hollyhock. This was a Native American remedy.

The pulverized flower of a painted daisy spread on the skin is an effective insect repellent.

The leaves of the herb feverfew made a fine medicinal tea for headache and fever.

Edible nasturtium flowers cured infections.

A tea of the herb yarrow is a fine drink to cure a cold and to wash a wound.

$\mathbb{C}$HAPTER 4

ROUTE 11: COLLINGWOOD TO CREEMORE AND DUNEDIN

- This route is good for cars, road and mountain bikes. There are some separate directions for road bikers so that we can keep you on the pavement. Mountain bikers can use either the car route, which covers some gravel roads, or the bike route.

You begin this journey in the flatter lands of Kirkville, MacMurchy's Settlement and Nottawa, and end in the vistas of lush hills and valleys of Creemore, Smithdale and Glen Huron.

Cars and road and mountain bikers may head south on the Osler Road.

The little hub of homes and businesses you see around Kirkville are all that remain of this late-1880s settlement that began when Robert Kirk opened a flour mill on the banks of Silver Creek. Soon Kirkville had a general store, post office, blacksmith, and settlers' homes, a Methodist Church and Union School Section 17.

Though many trails and roads had improved by the 1880s, travel was always difficult. A 10-kilometer journey along the rocky, rutted roads could take half a day. Most villages had a hotel or inn to accommodate weary travellers, and Kirkville was no exception.

As you ride south, look to your right and try to picture the fine old Royal Oak Hotel. Years ago it stood there, inviting travellers in for a good meal and a warm bed. Guests might include a stagecoach driver and his passengers, men from the wagon trains delivering goods between Barrie and Owen Sound, and perhaps one of the few families that could afford a night's stay while moving to their new home in Collingwood Township or beyond.

Creemore

Georgian Bay

Collingwood

Wasaga Beach

124

26 Stayner

26 Barrie

CREEMORE

Angus

Dunedin

Jail

Dunedin

Further south, as you cross the Poplar Sideroad, you will find MacMurchy's Settlement. This road was nonexistent when the brothers Duncan and Archibald MacMurchy came here in the 1843. To find their land they fought tangled brush and dense forest.

Settlers in the 1860s blazed a crude trail through the forest and cleared some land for farming. The first schoolhouse in Collingwood Township, a simple log house, was built on the southwest corner of the Poplar and Osler Roads. Children followed a blazed trail as far as Craigleith to attend. In 1883, the log structure was proudly replaced with the brick schoolhouse that stands on this corner today.

If you are travelling by mountain bike or car, continue past the Poplar Sideroad and follow the Osler Sideroad south to the Nottawasaga Sideroad. Follow this east into Nottawa. (For road bike directions, see below.)

 • **Great view.** The Osler Bluffs Road bends around and becomes Nottawa Sideroad. This rarely travelled road takes you through lovely scenery and past gorgeous homes, such as the second log home on the east side of the road. Built in the 1830s, this is one of the oldest log homes in the area.

If you are riding a road bike, stay on this road. At MacMurchy's Settlement, turn east off the Osler Bluffs Road onto the Poplar Sideroad. Follow this to Concession 10 and turn south. Follow Concession 10 to the Nottawasaga Sideroad, turn east, and go to Nottawa.

Throughout the mid-1800s, this village was known as Nottawa Mills. Huge sawmills and grist mills on the banks of the Pretty River brought new business and prosperity. A pioneer could complete many tasks with one trip to Nottawa Mills.

Imagine Nottawa in the fall of 1865. You and the other farmers are bringing the corn harvest to the grist mill to be ground into

112

meal. Prosperous families have come by ox and wagon. Others rely on the generosity of more established neighbours to loan transportation. A few carry loads on their backs, going back and forth as many times as possible before winter.

The barter system is alive and well in Nottawa and Upper Canada. After grinding the corn, you leave some at the mill as payment, and set some aside for the neighbour who kindly loaned his wagon. Some is traded in the village for blacksmith work perhaps, or cloth from the weaver, or boots and seed from the general store. Maybe you can afford sugar for baking or candy for the children.

Just south of the bridge into Nottawa, the general store still stands. A huge, redbrick building, the Pretty River General Store stands as a witness to prosperity. Built in 1865, the store is "older than Canada itself," and as filled with history, says present owner Robert King.

Native and European trappers came to the store with beaver and fox pelts for sale or trade. Three taverns and four hotels in the village made it easy for these men to celebrate their newfound wealth. Sometimes the celebration ended in fights and vandalism. Canada was not yet a country with police and laws. The owner of the general store had an ingenious way of surviving. Expecting trouble, he turned the long cranks that raised large wooden shutters over each window, protecting his property from the brawls in the night. Those cranks so nervously turned over 130 years ago are still there, in the bakery of the general store, and the huge shutters they raised are in the basement.

Cars and road and mountain bikes all head south on County Road 124 from Nottawa and turn east onto the local airport road. Follow it through the first Stop sign and go to the Fairgrounds Road, and turn south. You can also reach this route from Duntroon.

This is agricultural Ontario, with fields surrounded by split-rail and barbed-wire fences, brick farmhouses set back from the road,

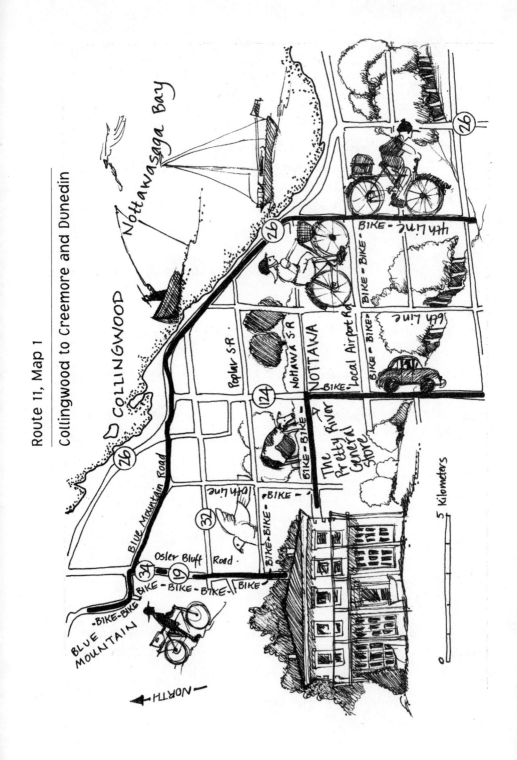

Route 11, Map 1

Collingwood to Creemore and Dunedin

114

Route 11, Map 2

Collingwood to Creemore and Dunedin

and enormous barns. The grandchildren and great-grandchildren of the original settlers who steadfastly cleared the rocks and stumps still own many of these farms.

 • **Great view.** Osler Bluffs rises behind farmland to the west of Fairgrounds Road and to the south the hills dissolve into the sky.

Cars and road and mountain bikes cross Highway 91 and continue south on Fairgrounds Road, which we will call by its pioneer name, the 4th Line.

As you cross Highway 91, the landscape south of the highway seems lusher, greener. Was it because most of the settlers here came from the Emerald Isle? This stretch of Fairgrounds Road was once known as the Irish Settlement.

Notice the East Nottawasaga Presbyterian Church. Built of log in 1854, the church was bricked over in 1881 with the original structure beneath. Many buildings over a century old have been torn down or ravaged by fire through the years, but this church, with its pioneer cemetery, is precious and unique.

Another small and lonely cemetery is further south at the Irish Settlement. Grave markers date from 1836 when tens of thousands of Irish reached Canada's shores. Famine, disease, overpopulation, political upheaval and over-taxation based on tithes made life for Ireland's poor miserable. Ocean crossings weren't much better. The converted lumber ships that brought the Irish immigrants were wretched. But the Irish of the 19th century risked everything to survive in the New World.

The earliest settlers arrived at Nottawasaga in the 1830s. Their cemetery attests to the hardships they endured; many of these markers are those of children. This was the first Catholic cemetery in the southern Georgian Bay area. A Catholic church and a small log schoolhouse were built here. Nearby settlers were nearly all

Protestant, but the Irish settlement thought it important to educate their children about their Catholic heritage.

Eventually, a public school was built nearby, and in 1855, the two schools combined for economic reasons. The Catholic school was later torn down along with the church.

Life in Canada wasn't easy for these Irish children. The political and religious troubles from home followed them across the miles of ocean to the public school on the 4th Line. Rivalries and animosity resulted in verbal and physical fights. One school inspector described what he saw in the classroom thus: "Some studying, but most sleeping. Teacher leaving doesn't care." But parents would not be deterred from ensuring an education for their children.

When James Currie offered to sell the School Section a quarter acre of land for 25 dollars, the settlers built a large frame schoolhouse. Just down the road from the Irish Settlement, on the east side, you'll find Nottawasaga S.S. 2, a brick schoolhouse that replaced the frame one in 1884.

The lonely Catholic cemetery with its few gravestones standing in a row was too wet to be properly maintained, and was eventually moved one concession west. The grave markers on the west side of Fairgrounds Road show the original location of that cemetery.

All travellers may continue south on the 4th Line (Fairgrounds Road).

Five hundred years ago, this land was forest. Late in the 15th century, the Petun nation came north from the Humber Valley to live here, in and around what we now call Creemore. Game was plentiful. The Petun cut clearings for their villages, some up to fifteen acres in size, and for fields in which they grew corn, beans, squash and sunflowers. Wood from clearing the land was used to construct the longhouses and palisades and was also used as fuel for cooking fires. Smoke from the continuously burning fires of the Petun signalled to the Huron living near Midland and Penetang that others lived along the shoreline to the south. The Huron called them "the people in the hills."

A village usually had three entrances in its palisade walls. Within the walls were longhouses built for each family, a longhouse for the main chief, visitors quarters, and garbage pits. The longhouse had two small rooms at each end for entry and store areas. Firepits ran down the middle of the house with bunks down each side.

Each longhouse accommodated large, extended families that descended from the female line. Upon marrying, the man moved into his wife's family longhouse. His children traced their heritage through her.

Cooperation and sharing among relatives were crucial to the Petun. Problem solving and decision making were democratically practised at all levels of society, including in the longhouse. Decisions were made by consensus. In the larger groups, when the whole village, nation, or confederacy was involved, the best orator made announcement of the final decision. In the longhouse, that job fell to the eldest woman, the matriarch. Most of the First Nations practised a far superior form of democracy than we see today.

Although the Petun arrived in the Creemore area when they first came north, they spread their villages along the shoreline as far as Kimberley and Thornbury. Archaeologists have registered 92 villages, making this the most important archaeological region in Ontario. Villages are scattered along the Blue Mountain and Osler Roads, and more have been found along the ridge near the Osler Bluffs Ski Club. Their trails leading from the villages down to the water can still be found today.

Cars and road and mountain bikes may head down the steep winding hill, over Simcoe Road 9 and onto Creemore's main street, Mill Street.

Only one word does justice to the village of Creemore: picturesque. The streets, covered by an archway of shade trees, are lined with fine old homes and buildings. In the first block south of Simcoe, look to the west side of the road for one of the few remaining hitching posts in Ontario. A century ago, Mill Street was a wide dirt path or, depending on the weather, a muddy trail. Nearly every home at this end had a unique hitching post. On the east side, they were thick posts of wood, three to four feet high with a hole drilled near the top. On the west side, however, the posts were shorter, fancier, and made of iron.

Creemore began in 1842 as a group of lots set aside by the government for the United Empire Loyalists. One of its earliest arrivals was Mr. Webster, whose family came by boat. Most settlers left the water behind upon reaching the shores of the Bay, travelling inland on foot. Not so the Websters.

The Welland Canal had just been completed. The Websters left Brockville, sailed through Lakes Erie, St. Clair, and Huron, then into the Bay. Reaching the mouth of the Nottawasaga River, Mr. Webster decided he'd continue by water. He walked only the final few miles to his destination.

The Webster family became such important members of the Creemore community that many of the streets in town are named after the Webster children.

Creemore itself became a village of firsts. In 1854, St. Luke's became the first Church of England established in Nottawasaga Township. In 1883, Creemore became the first police village in

Simcoe County, and in 1892 they built the jail claimed as the smallest in North America.

The best first came in the 1920s. When the sun began to set on Saturdays, those in the know waited for Mr. E. H. Nichol. Mr. Nichol, a tailor by trade, set a movie projector above his shop. On the opposite rooftop, he'd set up a screen. When the sky darkened, the show began. Black-and-white images flickered across the screen. Harold Lloyd swung from the hands of that famous clock; Chaplin's little tramp was in trouble again. This was, perhaps, the world's first drive-in theatre.

Creemore is a Gaelic word that means "big heart," a claim the village lives up to today.

- **Be sure to visit the Creemore Brewery.**

- **North America's smallest jail** is one block east of Mill Street. An elfin 15 by 20 feet, this stone structure is a reminder of pioneer justice.

The jail was built in 1892, at a time when judges, or squires as they were known, travelled from town to town dispensing "pioneer justice." The squire's visits were few and far between. Many disputes were cleared up before the judge arrived.

So few people lived in this area, crime was unusual. But when a crime occurred, tempers flared, one person charged another, and the wait for the squire commenced. More often than not, the problem was solved when the defendant cooled down, made amends, or the dispute was forgotten altogether. If this was impossible, the magistrates arranged a meeting between the accused and his alleged victim.

A tavern, usually the largest place in town, often served as the courtroom. The mayor, a minister or prominent community member served as mediator. The accused and accuser brought any witnesses. After both sides of the story were heard, matters were settled then and there. With so few jails in early Canada, a prison sentence was rare. Nine years after becoming the first policed village in Simcoe County, however, Creemore decided it needed a jail.

Needless to say, the tiny Creemore Jail — with three tiny cells, bunk, chamber pots, and sinks — had few famous criminals. The first occupant was an unjustly sentenced black cow who served time one November night in 1892. Most prisoners slept off a night of drinking. More serious offenders were sent to the jail in Dingwall, now called Stayner.

The Creemore Jail was a simple hotel during the 1930s Depression. Transients slept here, each permitted only one night in the jail, but each was given a food allowance. The Creemore jail was closed in the 1940s.

From the corner of Mill Street and Simcoe Road 9, head west on Simcoe Road 9. At the 6th Line, turn north at the Glen Huron sign, and ascend the long hill towards Smithdale.

- **Picnic spot.** Just before heading towards Glen Huron, take the time to visit Dunedin, a rare jewel of a community.

Follow Simcoe Road 9 west from Mill Street in Creemore, around the bend into town. The Knox United Church stands guard at the entrance to town; its picnic tables offer quiet, relaxing place.

Dunedin is the oldest settlement in Nottawasaga Township. Israel Bowerman came here in 1834. Perhaps his spirit gives the village a feeling of first discovery. Imagine being the first person to see the river winding through the solitude of thick, lush forest.

It was first known as Bowerman's Hollow, though others called it the Yankee Settlement, as it became a well-known destination for United Empire Loyalists fleeing the northeastern United States. Mr. John J. Carruthers renamed Dunedin after his hometown, Dunedin, New Zealand, to which he soon returned.

After your picnic, drive or cycle back along Simcoe Road 9 (you're now heading back towards Creemore) until you reach the 6th Line. Turn north onto the 6th Line.

- **Side trip.** Drive through Dunedin and around the bend on Simcoe Road 9 west to find craftspeople and Belhaven Antiques.

- **Great view.** The 6th Line is a classic winding road. The farm at the foot of the 6th Line and Simcoe Road 9 is built like a bookcase with three shelves. Clearing this rugged land without modern equipment took hard work and ingenuity. The road, through cedar forest and stone, passes swamps and bulrushes. Each bend brings a vista. In the deep gorge on the west, the Mad River tumbles to meet the Noisy River, which passes into Creemore.

- **Great view.** Nearing the top of this long hill, stop to look back to the south; we call this magical view of green forest, rolling fields, and red farmhouses the Emerald Valley.

At the Stop sign at the corner of the 6th Line and Sideroad 15-16, in Smithdale, turn west. This is for cars and road and mountain bikes.

Smithdale once played big brother to Glen Huron, whose residents came here for their mail and their basic needs. The village was named after the Smiths who came here in 1837. They followed a barely blazed trail through Stayner to Duntroon, then turned southeast to find their way here. When the Toronto, Simcoe and Lake Huron Railway Company brought its line from Toronto north to Collingwood, it stopped at Smithdale. The village already had lumber and stockyards, a grain house and a hotel.

On the north side of Sideroad 15-16 you'll find the Hamilton Brothers' Temperance Creek Farm, named for the nearby creek. No one knows if the man who named this creek was a priest or an extremely devout man. He went to the creek each morning, rain or shine, winter and summer, to bathe. He always carried a torch to scare off lurking wolves. He advised the people of Smithdale to drink the water daily, which he claimed was healing. An abstainer, he named the water Temperance Creek.

The Hamilton brothers were important businessmen to both Smithdale and Glen Huron. Settling in the 1870s, they began their dynasty. The roof of one barn in Glen Huron proudly states Hamilton Brothers Established in 1874. By 1895, James Hamilton owned the general store, was the loans master and postmaster for Glen Huron and, with his sons, owner of a flour mill, sawmill, shingle mill and planing mill. One glance around Glen Huron proves the Hamilton family is still of great importance to this village.

At the Stop sign just past the Glen Huron Memorial Chapel, turn north off Simcoe Road 62 and head up the hill towards Simcoe Road 124. At Highway 24, turn east to Duntroon.

- **Look on the map for the Bruce Trail.**

- **Picnic spot.** Just south of the turn onto Simcoe Road 124, a small provincial park overlooks the steep slopes of the Devil's Glen Ski Club.

Just north of the crossroads at Highways 91 and 124 in Duntroon (past the flashing light), you'll find a sign for the Sydenham Trail, a short remaining section of the Old Mail Road from Barrie to Owen Sound. Travellers headed to points west followed this road when they came to Smithdale, but most would have carried on to Rob Roy rather than turning south, as the Smiths did.

Duntroon began as 79 five-acre lots laid out in a square (see the map at the Pioneer Cemetery). The government purposely set these lots aside for settlement of the needy, with one lot given to each qualifying family member over the age of 21.

Although some settlers from Ireland and Germany came here, most came from Scotland, hence Duntroon was originally known as Scotch Corners. These disparate groups, with different languages and ignorance of each other's customs, somehow learned to communicate and cooperate for their survival.

When they arrived in the New World, they had no money or knowledge of their chosen home. Settlers from northwestern Europe, where the lands had been stripped of their forests by the 6th century, knew nothing about clearing land. After government agents gave them brief lessons, these pioneers, poor as they were, were left to establish their lives in the Canadian wilderness.

Life was not easy in the bush. New arrivals slept in lean-tos or log shanties with dirt floors and moss chinking. Some slept beneath the trees. They made their own furniture and cooking utensils and began clearing their lots. Since they were unable to purchase oxen or horses, working with basic tools, most clearing was done with brute strength. Huge trees were felled with an axe then dragged away with rope or chain by the men. Logs became houses. Rocks were laboriously rolled aside using strong branches for leverage, and piled in rows as fences and boundaries.

Vegetables were grown as soon as a plot was cleared. Government provisions lasted only a short time. Among the stumps stubbornly rooted in the ground, potatoes and turnips were planted in soil hand-tilled with a hoe held in sore, tired hands.

During their first gruelling winter, many of the pioneers of Scotch Corners abandoned their lots, knowing they couldn't make it through the winter alive. Others became ill or starved to death. Enough survived that harrowing winter to establish this village, which they named Bowmore, but eventually became Duntroon.

The grandparents of Mr. Jay Blair, one of Duntroon's best-known citizens and its "last pioneer," lived along the Sydenham Trail, then called the Back Lane, in a house built on the north side

Highlands Nordic · Duntroon
Phone for trail fees (weekend and
mid-week passes for adults,
families and groups) 705·
444·5017
Groomed and track set ·
Classic and skate · Number
of trails = 4, totalling 17km
30% easy, 60% intermediate,
10% advanced ·
Facilities include: rentals, ski shop, repairs,
snack bar, waxing room, first aid, ski patrol,
and ski school ·
Owned by : Highlands Nordic Inc · Box
110, Duntroon LOM 1H0   705·444·5017

of the trail, just west of the cemetery. By the time young Jay was playing on his own, his grandparents were well established and the Back Lane provided him with his own little playground. Here, Jay rode the first pedal vehicle in the Township, an iron-wheeled tricycle lacking brakes.

Mr. Blair became a well-known author and historian. Upon his death, this "last pioneer" was one of the last to be buried in the Pioneer Cemetery. He was buried alongside other members of the Blair family.

Cars and road and mountain bikes follow Highway 24 back to Collingwood.

- **Great cross-country skiing** at Duntroon Highlands Nordic Resort, west off Simcoe Road 124 at the flashing light. The resort hosted the 1996 Special Olympics.

IT IS WELL KNOWN that beer is a popular beverage in Britain. It became so at a time when disease and plague scourged the country. The British recognized, too late for many, that by tossing germ-ridden clothing and mattresses into the country's waterways, they had poisoned the water supply. Most Brits stopped drinking water for fear of death.

This fear of drinking water came to Canada with the pioneers. Although Ontario water was fresh and safe, the pioneers had no way of knowing that and looked for other sources of refreshment. Most pioneers couldn't afford a cow or goat for milk, nor did they grow orchards for fruit juice. So they made beer. If they lacked the ingredients, they improvised.

Spruce beer required 50 drops of spruce oil, two quarts of boiled water, one quart plus a gill of molasses, three beaten eggs and a gill of yeast. It was strained, and let stand for two hours to marry the flavours — and then consumed.

Other brews included corn, ginger root, dandelions with hops (said to taste much like ale), or a mix of burdock, yellow dock, dandelion, sarsaparilla and spikenard. In most recipes, plants mixed with hops were claimed to make a fine-flavoured brew.

Maple beer was made by boiling sap down to vinegar, then adding a handful of hops, a touch of liquor and a bit of barm (yeast) for fermentation. An added flavouring of spruce sprigs or bruised ginger spiced up this brew.

Fortunately, these beers came out of their vats with an alcohol content of up to 15 percent. Eventually, enough land was cleared to grow barley and so beer could be brewed as it had been it Britain, with more control over flavour and alcohol content.

RECIPES

BAKED BEANS

1 cup dried navy beans
4 cups water
1 chopped onion
3 tbsp. blackstrap molasses

1 tsp. dry mustard
Dash salt and pepper
½ cup ketchup or tomato paste
2 tbsp. honey

Place the beans in large saucepan and cover with water. Soak beans overnight. Drain and replace with fresh water. Heat to boiling and boil for 2 minutes. Remove from the heat and let stand 1 hour, keeping beans covered with water.

Place beans back on burner and simmer 50 minutes covered (until tender). Do not boil or beans will split. Drain the beans, keeping the water.

Preheat oven to 325 F.

Put beans in a 2-quart pot or roasting pan and mix in onion. Stir together remaining ingredients with two cups of bean liquid and pour over the beans. Cover and bake three hours, removing the cover for the last hour adding liquid if necessary.

BEEF 'N' BEER STEW

½ bottle beer
1 lb stewing beef in 1-inch cubes
½ cup flour
2 tbsp. oil
1 large onion, chopped
2 cups fresh beans or peas
3 carrots, chopped
1 potato

1 sweet potato
3 stalks celery
½ turnip, pared and cubed
½ tsp. salt
Dash pepper
3 tbsp. cornstarch
Generous pinch of seasonings
(parsley, chives, tarragon)

Trim fat from meat, cut in cubes and roll cubes in flour. Brown meat in 2 tbsp. oil over medium heat. Add onions and sauté until transparent and add ½ bottle beer (or so). Simmer. Meanwhile chop vegetables; place in a large pot and cover with water. Bring to a boil until potatoes are cooked. Drain water. Add meat and simmer ½ hour. Mix cornstarch with cold water to make a paste and add to mixture to thicken.

Serves 4.

SWEET AND SOUR SPARE RIBS

1 cup ketchup
2 tbsp. Worcestershire sauce
1 tbsp. dry mustard
1 ½ tbsp. cider vinegar
2 tbsp. honey

2 cloves garlic, pressed
½ tsp. fresh pepper
3–4 lbs spareribs
2 onions thinly sliced

Combine first seven ingredients in a bowl and set aside.

Place ribs on rack in shallow roasting pan; bake uncovered in preheated 450 F oven 15 minutes. Add ½ inch of water if too dry.

Turn and bake 15 minutes longer.

Remove from oven; drain off drippings.

Reduce oven to 325 F, spoon half of the sweet and sour sauce over ribs and bake, uncovered, for 20 minutes.

Turn ribs and brush with remaining sauce; bake about 20 minutes until well glazed. (Cut meaty portion of rib to make sure no pink remains).

For the barbecue:

Place partially cooked ribs on the barbecue, brush sauce on and cook 10 minutes. Turn over and brush on remaining sauce and barbecue 10 minutes longer.

Serves 4.

EASY BEAN SALAD

1 can kidney beans
1 can chickpeas
1 can romano beans
1 can corn
½ red or green pepper, chopped
½ bunch green onions, chopped

DRESSING
1–2 cloves garlic, crushed
¼ cup vinegar
1 tsp. dried mustard
1 tsp. dill

Rinse and drain beans. Mix all ingredients in a bowl. Prepare dressing in a separate container. Pour over bean mixture and let sit for an hour or so. This salad tastes even better after marinating 24 hours.

Chicken in Tossed Salad

Take a wonderful loaf of bread to eat with this salad.

Barbecue or oven bake 2 lbs of boneless chicken and cut into ½-inch slices or cubes or slice precooked smoked ham into ½-inch slices or cubes.

Use your creativity.

Wash and spin dry a head of romaine lettuce or use half romaine and half spinach. Add a handful of any or all of the following:

Red cabbage, chopped
Red onion, sliced thinly
Grated carrot
Sliced radishes
Raisins
Pumpkin seeds
Tomatoes, sliced and diced
Sliced chicken or ham

DRESSING
1–2 cloves garlic, minced
¼ cup olive oil
¼ cup cider vinegar
½ tsp. mustard powder
1 pinch dill

Combine all ingredients in a jar and shake well. Pour over salad and toss, once you arrive at your picnic spot.

Serves 4–6.

Date Nuggets

1 egg
⅛ cup natural unrefined sugar
½ tsp. vanilla
8 oz. dates cut into small pieces

1 cup chopped walnuts
1 cup natural cereal with fruit and nuts
Natural sugar

Beat egg. Gradually beat in ⅛-cup sugar. Add vanilla. Add dates, walnuts and cereal to egg mixture, mixing well. Press evenly into buttered 8-inch square pan. Bake in 350 F oven 25 minutes or until lightly browned. Remove from oven and cool on wire rack about 10 minutes. While still warm, cut into 1-inch cubes. Remove one at a time and press into a ball. Roll immediately in sugar. When cool store in covered jar.

PEANUT BUTTER BALLS

1 cup honey
1 cup peanut butter

½ cup wheat germ
½ cup non-instant skim milk powder

Mix all ingredients together and roll into balls. Roll in coconut.

OATMEAL RAISIN COOKIES

½ cup butter
½ cup liquid honey (slightly
  warmed)
½ cup brown sugar
1 egg
1 cup whole-wheat flour

1 cup rolled oats
¼ cup wheat germ
1 tsp. baking powder
1 tsp. baking soda
1 ½ cup raisins

In a large bowl cream together, butter, honey, brown sugar and egg.
Add flour, oats, wheat germ, baking powder and baking soda. Mix well.
Stir in raisins. Drop by heaping teaspoons onto lightly greased baking
sheets. Flatten with fork. Bake in 325 F oven for 12–15 minutes or until
light golden.
   Makes 4 dozen.

TO AVOID BAD LUCK

Never cut a loaf of bread while holding it upside down.

Never eat fruit that grew in a graveyard.

Avoid white corn shoots, white cabbage heads, and white beans as
   a sign of impending troubles.

Never eat the fruit of a blackberry bush that has blossomed immediately after another crop has been picked from that bush.

CHAPTER 5

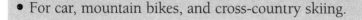

ROUTE 12: COLLINGWOOD TO MIDLAND

- For car, mountain bikes, and cross-country skiing.

We suggest you drive to Midland by the shortest route to allow time to savour the historical and natural sites, then meander back along the shoreline. The drive from Collingwood to Midland encompasses a variety of scenes, from the raucous beach community of Wasaga to farmland and small villages. Midland has a small-town look, feels like cottage country, and is steeped in history.

Begin on Highway 26 out of Collingwood, and follow Highway 26 to the lights at Mosley Street. Turn north on Mosley towards Wasaga. At the fork of Mosley Street and River Road, follow River Road northeast towards Elmvale. River Road becomes Highway 92.

- **Great cross-country skiing and hiking.** At the Wasaga end of Highway 92, watch on the south side for Wasaga Beach Provincial Park and Blueberry Trails for cross-country skiing or hiking.

- **Don't miss the Elmvale Flea Market.** After leaving Wasaga, watch on the north side of Highway 92 for the Elmvale Flea Market, where you'll discover a mix of kitsch, fresh fruits, vegetables and baking. Local farmers auction their livestock in the barn. Open Thursday and Saturday.

Continue on Highway 92 to the lights in Elmvale and turn left (north) onto Highway 27. Follow Highway 27 around the bend northeast towards Waverly. Just before Waverly, turn north on Highway 93 through Wyebridge and follow the signs to Midland.

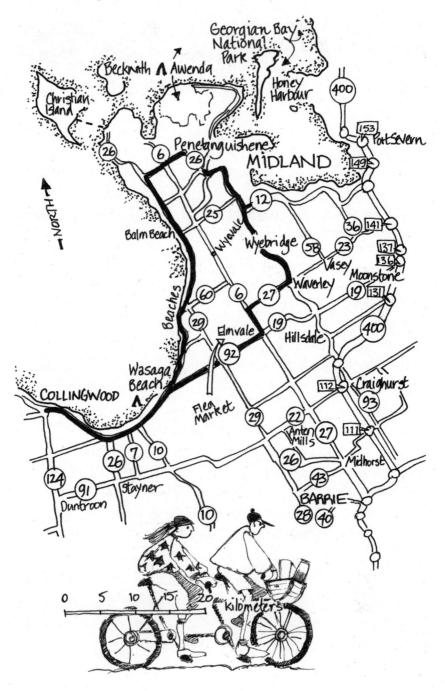

Ⓐ Kilometer 0.0 : Oakview Community Centre · Park · Start ·
Turn left on to Mosley st ·
Ⓑ Kilometer 1.4 : Stay right and follow River Rd· W ·
Ⓒ Kilometer 7.0 : Turn left on to Zoo Park Rd ·
Ⓓ Kilometer 8.3 : At stop sign turn right ·
Ⓔ Kilometer 9.5: Turn left, following "New Wasaga
Beach / Allen wood Beach" signs ·
Ⓕ Kilometer 11.6 : At stop sign, turn right, then left ·
Ⓖ Kilometer 14.3 : Turn right then left · Look for
"Tiny Beaches" sign ·
Ⓗ Kilometer 16.6 : sharp
bend to right, then again ·
Ⓘ Kilometer 18.1 : at next
stop sign turn right ·
Ⓙ Kilometer 19.4 : turn left
Head around sharp right ·
at Ⓚ Kilometer 27 · then
follow "one way" sign to
stop · This is Balm Beach ·

Midland

Balm Beach
Ossossane Beach
Wymbolwood Beach
Wendake Beach
Bluewater Beach
Deanlea Beach
Woodland Beach

Elmvale

Nottawasaga Bay

Thornbury

Wasaga Beach

Collingwood

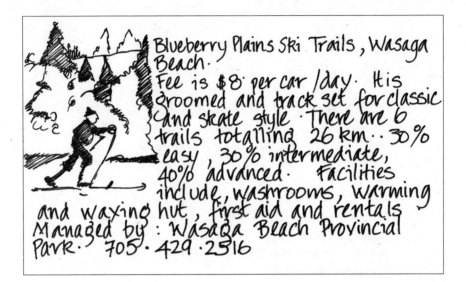

Blueberry Plains Ski Trails, Wasaga Beach.
Fee is $8 per car/day. It is groomed and track set for classic and skate style. There are 6 trails totalling 26 km. 30% easy, 30% intermediate, 40% advanced. Facilities include, washrooms, warming and waxing hut, first aid and rentals Managed by: Wasaga Beach Provincial Park. 705·429·2516

- **Great hiking, biking, cross-country skiing.** The first "rails to trails" conversion in Ontario runs along County Road 6, which ends 22 kilometers later in Penetanguishene. The trail is accessed in Wyevale Park, a few kilometers northwest on County Road 6 from Elmvale. The trail passes through hardwood forest, open fields and the rolling greens of a golf course, where yellow warblers, blue jays, orioles and bobolinks nest in the treetops. The historic site of the Ossosane Native Burial Pit is a good stop with ample parking.

- **Great picnic spot.** The little village of Wyebridge on the edge of the Wye River has many beautiful old buildings, shops and a restaurant. Look around, have a picnic and an ice cream cone.

Midland and the Huron Nation

The ancestors of the Huron nation lived on the southern and eastern shores of Georgian Bay as early as AD 500. Evidence shows the natives of these lands grew corn and built permanent villages with palisades and longhouses. By AD 1000 this agricultural nation had added tobacco and beans to their fields and, within another two hundred years, sunflowers and squash. Corn remained the important crop for the Huron nation, as it travelled well when dried and was a perfect commodity for trade with nations to the south and west.

During these years of agricultural growth, the Huron and other Iroquoian-speaking people developed a sophisticated society, divided into nations. Each nation was made up of many villages with a number of clans, or families.

Although the Huron did not believe in status linked to personal property or the size of one's family, they did believe that it could be gained through committing brave actions in battle. Long ago, battles were defensive. If a group travelled over a trade route without obtaining permission, a small raiding party would stop them. Battles were short, with little bloodshed, few deaths, and perhaps prisoners taken. Sometimes captives were adopted into a clan.

By the 15th and 16th centuries, the Iroquois of the St. Lawrence region and the Huron battled over territory claimed by the French and English. Tradition demanded revenge by relatives of the warriors killed in battle. To make or keep peace, the warrior who killed offered compensation to the family of the dead warrior. Sometimes compensation was not enough and fighting continued. The women of the clan or village decided when and if warriors went into battle.

The Huron people were deeply spiritual. They believed spirits were in the birds, fish, and animals, in the sky, in the rocks, in the rivers. The spirits and the physical world were one and the same. As a people, the Huron were relatives of the animals and plants around them.

The most powerful influence in their lives was the Sky Spirit, which controlled the weather and helped humans in need. Lesser spirits influenced the daily life and interrelations of people. Called Oki, these spirits were respected both publicly and privately with the help of a shaman, or Healer. Unlike the Ojibwa, the Huron believed wise men or women could interpret the signs, visions and dreams sent by the spirits. The Huron believed illness occurred from natural causes, sorcery, or unfulfilled desires. The Healer's special relationship with his personal Oki revealed dreams and visions, and the causes of illness.

Unfortunately, the Healers could not cure measles, smallpox, and influenza after the arrival of the Europeans. Sainte-Marie-Among-the-Hurons was the first European settlement in Ontario. The Jesuit priests who inhabited it were convinced of their good deeds as they changed the face of the Huron Nation forever.

Over two hundred years later, in 1872, Midland took shape. Known in the 1830s and 1840s as a loose farming settlement called Mundy's Bay or Hartley's Landing, the area became established when the Midland Railway Company from Peterborough and Port Hope decided to make use of its good harbour. Meanwhile, the Midland Land Company bought 400 acres of land from a group of settlers and had it surveyed as a townsite. The proposed town was named Midland City.

The train line brought rapid growth to Midland City, which was officially incorporated as Midland in 1890. The town increased steadily in size and prestige while maintaining its important historical past. Few small towns in Ontario, let alone Canada, have done such a superlative job of presenting history in an exciting and informative way. Murals painted on the sides of the buildings depict

Collingwood to Midland

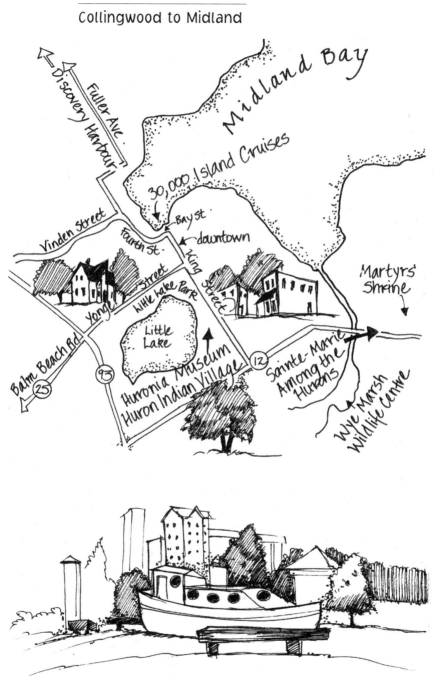

scenes from Sainte-Marie-Among-the-Hurons, the wildlife of the Wye Marsh, and the sawmill, farming, and daily life of Midland of the past century.

The best way to learn of the amazing history that surrounds Midland is to visit the many historical sights.

Huronia Museum and Huron Indian Village

Located at Little Lake Park in Midland, this replica Huron village demonstrates how the Huron lived for more than two thousand years. Outside the palisades, cornfields ripen. At the entrance to the village, symbolic masks announce which families are home. Longhouses, wigwams, sweat lodges, drying racks and fire pits and reenactments of both the spiritual and physical aspects of this culture depict this lost way of life.

The Huronia Museum, on the same site, displays artifacts over a span of 11,000 years, from prehistory to modern-day memorabilia, and features art from the people of Huronia.

Sainte-Marie-Among-the-Hurons

Sainte-Marie-Among-the-Hurons was the first European settlement in Ontario, founded by the French Jesuits in 1639 as a mission for itinerant missionaries and Christian Hurons. The Jesuits brought livestock from Quebec and became self-sufficient with the help of the Huron people. Structures were built, vegetable gardens planted and the mission appeared to prosper.

Outside the palisades of Sainte-Marie-Among-the-Hurons, however, resentment and anger grew among the Huron as they watched influenza, measles and smallpox brought by the Jesuits kill thousands of their people.

In July of 1648, the traditional wars of the Huron and Iroquois rekindled. The Iroquois captured and killed many Huron and Jesuits, including Father Jean de Brebeuf. The people of Sainte-Marie-Among-the-Hurons, exhausted from waiting for an attack, set fire to the mission and travelled by canoe to Christian Island.

Other Huron travelled along the shoreline (some say across the ice of the bay) to ask the Petun to take them in. Although their numbers tripled the population of some villages, the Petun fed and housed them as best they could. After a winter of hardship and starvation at Sainte-Marie II on Christian Island, the Jesuits abandoned their mission completely, returning to Quebec with a few hundred Christian Huron in 1650.

The Sainte-Marie-Among-the-Hurons village is an accurate recreation with well-informed guides in period costume. Inside the palisades are the Jesuit mission and native encampment furnished and perfectly detailed. You can visit a longhouse, see moccasins being made and corn pounded, or visit the blacksmith's shop and watch him pound the nails that repair the buildings. You can look out over the gardens, visit the simple living quarters of the priests and view some of the original stone fireplaces constructed over three hundred years ago.

- **Martyr's Shrine.** The magnificent Martyr's Shrine, high on a hill, was built in 1926 in memory of the Jesuit priests and two lay people martyred during the mid-1600s. Father de Brebeuf's grave is on the grounds.

- **Discovery Harbour.** Although Discovery Harbour is in Penetang, it is close enough to Midland for a quick visit. The harbour is a marine heritage site with replicas of the historic tall ships H.M.S. *Bee* and H.M.S. *Tecumseth*. Guides show you through this British naval outpost (1817–1856) and through the replica of the officer's quarters circa 1845.

- **Wye Marsh Wildlife Centre.** Located near Sainte-Marie-Among-the-Hurons, the centre offers guided tours dedicated to the trumpeter swan, turtles, water bugs and other aspects of the marsh. Call ahead.

- **30,000 Islands Boat Cruise.** Sail through the waters of Georgian Bay's east shore, home of the windswept, rocky and beautiful 30,000 Islands.

The three-hundred-seat *Miss Midland* leaves Midland Town Dock for a two-and-a-half-hour cruise past Honey Harbour, rounds tree-covered Little Beausoleil Island, and sails into open waters for the return trip. It's a great way to view the natural beauty that inspired the members of the Group of Seven.

After enjoying the sights of Midland, you have two choices. If you are short on time, return the way you came. Otherwise, follow us!

From Midland, by bike or car, follow Simcoe Road 29, also called the Tiny Beaches Road. We begin in Balm Beach and head south to Wasaga.

- **Great mountain bike route, with many picnic spots.** Balm Beach is the essence of cottage country. Here, a cottage is a cottage, not a monster home, and narrow sandy roads wind though the woods.

A building that epitomizes this summer feeling is Lawson's Amusements, opened by Vera Lawson and her husband in the early 1950s. Meant to be a pool hall, the business grew to include a lunch and ice-cream counter, and an amusement area with pinball machines and more. Though the business no longer exists, the building, with its Insulbrick exterior and faded signs reading Billiards, Snooker, Ice Cream and Cigarettes, is a magnificent sight, suggesting damp sand, suntan lotion and water of the bay even in winter.

Across from the amusement hall sits another fascinating building. Originally built in Elmvale by an early pioneer, this pioneer home is over 130 years old. In 1939, Edgar Lawson bought this old cabin. With his two sons, he dismantled the house, painstakingly marking each log, board and piece of trim as he went. Using horses and a wagon as well as a truck, Mr. Lawson moved the whole house to Balm Beach and rebuilt it like a puzzle. It served as a

summer home for decades, and the Lawson family eventually moved permanently to Balm Beach.

As you ride the beach roads of Wasaga Beach, consider this: when settlers arrived in the mid-1800s, this land could not be sold even for twenty-five cents an acre. What farmer dependent upon a good crop wanted miles of sand?

The river tells even more tales. The name of the Nottawasaga River comes from the Iroquois and Petun word *nottaway*, which means "snake," and *saga*, which means "mouth of the river." During the uprisings of the mid-1600s, the Iroquois used this river to steal upon the Petun nation, so it became the Nottawasaga, or "the mouth of the river where the snakes come from."

A century and a half later, during the War of 1812, the river was used for military purposes. The schooner *Nancy* was sent from Kingston, sailing through Lake Simcoe and into Georgian Bay to bring supplies to the British troops at Fort Michilimackinac. The fort, an important trading post located where Lakes Michigan and

Huron join, was captured from the Americans who cut it off from supplies.

With only 23 crew and 3 guns, the *Nancy* was sunk by an American brig and two schooners, heavily armed with, in all, 500 crew and 24 guns. They discovered the *Nancy* hiding among the trees about 2 miles up the Nottawasaga River. Her hull, burned to the waterline, rests at the Nancy Island Museum.

During the lumbering era, in the late 1800s, the Nottawasaga River was an important transportation route. When the lands were cleared of all trees, a new era began.

By the turn of the century, residents of nearby Stayner, Duntroon, Elmvale and Collingwood began to cottage here. They came by horse and buggy to summer on the banks of the river, rarely venturing to the Bay. With new interest in the area around 1918, entre-preneurs began building resorts, guest cottages, nightclubs and other tourist facilities on both the river and the Bay.

By the 1930s, people arrived in the thousands for beach week-ends. Cars parked on the sand as their owners spent the day on the longest freshwater beach in the world. By night, the sounds of some of the best-known big bands of the time wafted through the air. Wasaga Beach hit its stride, and no one would ever say its sandy soil was useless again.

In 1934 the first non-stop flight from Canada to Britain began here. Using the beach as a natural runway, the pilot guided his DeHaviland Dragon biplane across the sands and then into the sky to begin his epic journey.

The Wasaga Beach of today hasn't changed much in sixty years. Although you can no longer park on the sand, you can spend your day on that long, long beach, listen to some of Canada's best bands by night, and have a great time, along with thousands of others, being a part of the modern cottage era.

- **The Nancy Island Museum.** Located on Mosley Street just north of the fork to River Road. This museum is dedicated to the history of the Nancy, the schooner sunk by the Americans during the War of 1812.

- **The beach is a great picnic spot, with parking, facilities, and viewpoints along the water.**

RECIPES

ROASTED CHICKEN

1 roasting chicken (wild turkey or
  any fowl)

Preheat oven to 375 F. Place chicken in roasting pan breast side down, and cook for one hour. Remove chicken from pan. Drain off excess fat; add 2 cups of water or stock to pan, and stir, scraping brown glaze from bottom of pan. Turn chicken breast side up; replace in pan and continue cooking 30 minutes, baste with sauce.
  Serves 4.

BREAD STUFFING FOR FOWL

We don't always have time to stuff our fowl, but here is an easy recipe for those special times.

9 cups soft bread crumbs　　　*3 medium minced onions*
1 ½ tsp. salt　　　*½ cup butter*
¾ tsp. sage　　　*2 medium gizzards (optional)*
½ tsp. pepper

Mix bread crumbs, seasonings and onions. Melt butter and pour over crumbs tossing lightly with a fork. Chopped celery, corn or chestnuts may be added in place of gizzards.

LEFTOVERS CHICKEN SOUP

Chicken carcass, stripped of all meat　　　*2 carrots*
  (reserve meat)　　　*2 stalks celery*
1 medium onion, chopped　　　*Any leftover vegetables*

Put carcass in a large kettle and cover with water. Add onions, carrots, celery and chicken meat. Bring to a boil, reduce heat, and simmer on very low heat for 3 hours. Remove bones from broth. (I usually let soup sit overnight and skim the fat in the morning.) Use your favourite spices . . . try curry, salt and pepper.
  Serve bannock with this soup instead of dumplings or bread.

BANNOCK

2 ½ cups all-purpose flour
5 tsp. baking powder
½ tsp. salt
2 tbsp. sugar
3 tbsp. lard (or butter, oil makes it
    heavy)

1 egg (optional)
1 cup water
Add raisins or fresh berries
    (optional).

Combine flour, baking powder, salt and sugar in bowl. Add lard. Rub in to form fine crumbs. If using egg, combine with water. Add to flour mixture. Stir to form soft dough. Knead until smooth, about 10 seconds.

Lightly grease heavy cast iron skillet with lard. (I use a greased 9 x 9-inch square pan.) Dust with flour. Place dough in pan and bake in a 350 F oven for 40 minutes.

BROCCOLI SALAD

1 bunch of broccoli florets (2–3 cups)
½ cup chopped red onion
¼ cup pumpkin seeds, sunflower
    seeds or walnuts
½ cup Thompson raisins
½ cup feta cheese, crumbled

YOGURT DRESSING
¾ cup low-fat yogurt
2 tbsp. liquid honey (slightly
    warmed)
A squeeze of lemon juice

Combine first five ingredients in a bowl. Stir together yogurt dressing ingredients in jar. Mix well. Pour over salad and toss. Serves four.

This salad will keep several days in the refrigerator.

BASIL HONEY CHICKEN

⅓ cup butter or margarine
3 tsp. basil, dried
1 tsp. mustard powder
1–2 cloves garlic, crushed

½ cup honey
2 tbsp. vinegar
4 chicken breasts, skinned

Combine first six ingredients in an uncovered casserole dish. Place chicken in this mixture. Bake at 400 F for 45 minutes. Baste frequently.

Great served over a rice dish.

GRAIN SALAD

1 cup pot barley
2–2 ½ cups chicken stock
1 tbsp. butter
1 cup onion, chopped fine
1 cup mushrooms, sliced

½ cup carrots, diced
¾ cup raisins
½ cup frozen peas
½ cup sunflower seed

Bring chicken stock to a boil and add pot barley. Simmer on low until barley has absorbed all liquid (30–40 minutes). Melt butter in a skillet. Cook onion, mushrooms and carrots until onion is transparent. Put aside. Add to cooked barley. Add raisins, peas and sunflower seeds. Mix well.

This can be eaten warm or cold.

BUTTERMILK BRAN MUFFINS

3 eggs
¼ cup honey
⅓ cup vegetable oil
¼ cup molasses
2 cups bran
1 cup grated carrot
1 cup mashed bananas or pureed
   fruit

1 ½ cups buttermilk
1 ½ cups whole wheat flour
½ cup wheat germ
1 tsp. baking soda
2 tsp. baking powder
1 tsp. salt
½ cup raisins

In large bowl, beat eggs, honey, oil and molasses until fluffy. Add carrot, banana and buttermilk. Stir well. In separate bowl, mix flour, wheat germ, soda, baking powder, salt and raisins. Add to egg mixture and stir only to moisten. Put in greased muffin tins.

Bake at 350 F for 20–25 minutes.

Makes 12.

PRESERVATION

IN THE PIONEER DAYS, smoked meat was packed in a variety of innovative ways. Pulverized charcoal could keep smoked hams for months, even years.

Beef was often pickled. A recipe for one hundred pounds of beef called for seven pounds of salt, one ounce each of saltpetre and cayenne pepper, one quart of molasses, and eight gallons of soft water. The mixture was boiled, skimmed, and poured over the beef.

To keep meat fresh for one or two weeks, even in warm weather, it was placed in a pan of sour milk or buttermilk and kept cool, and then rinsed well before cooking.

CHAPTER 6

ROUTE 13: COLLINGWOOD TO THE BRUCE PENINSULA

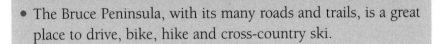

- The Bruce Peninsula, with its many roads and trails, is a great place to drive, bike, hike and cross-country ski.

The Bruce Peninsula deserves as much time as you can give. The drive from Collingwood to Tobermory is about two hours. The Bruce demands at least a daytrip, or better, a weekend, either camping or at one of the many bed and breakfasts.

From Collingwood, head west towards Owen Sound on Highway 26, which ends at the lights in Owen Sound, at the Junction of Highway 26 and Highway 6 & 10. Turn south onto Highway 6 & 10, and follow it to the first set of lights. Turn west onto Highway 21, and drive through Owen Sound, up a steep hill on the west side of the town. Continue straight on Highway 21 to the lights at Highway 70 and the sign that says Shallow Lake. Turn north, and follow Highway 70 to the lights at Highway 6 & 10. Turn north. Highway 6 leads to Tobermory at the tip of the Bruce Peninsula.

From the 1400s into the 1600s, the Bruce Peninsula was inhabited by members of the Algonkian-speaking Ottawa nation who, mostly because of the Iroquois wars, were moving north, eventually to settle on Manitoulin Island. In the late 1700s, a native band occupied the Peninsula again. Like the Ottawa, the Ojibwa are an amalgamation of Algonkian-speaking Anishnabe, or kindred people. The Ojibwa are the last natives on the Peninsula, where many still reside, and the last in the southern Georgian Bay region.

The Ojibwa and their descendants lived in Ontario, which they called Saganan, where they hunted, fished, and gathered plants.

Samuel de Champlain described the Ojibwa as the *cheveaux releves,* or "high hairs," and "they wear no breech cloths and are much carved about the body in divisions of various patterns. They paint their faces . . . have their nostrils pierced and their ears fringed with beads."

Having close alliances with other Alkonkian-speaking nations, the Ojibwa welcomed natives from other bands into their communities. This unselfish attitude prevailed throughout the Ojibwa culture. Jobs were done well simply to do them well, personal possessions shared, and orphans quickly adopted.

Ojibwa leaders were appointed and came to the forefront only during times of crisis. Decisions were made by consensus and all were heard. In emergencies, orders and commands were never issued. Thus the Ojibwa often appeared leaderless. As warriors, the Ojibwa were brilliant at guerrilla-style warfare, striking suddenly, and then quietly disappearing into the forest.

The Ojibwa looked within for spiritual guidance. Each person knew his inner self and from a young age was versed in the spiritual ways. Armed with a long, thin club, or bow and arrow, a hunter or warrior's skills of speed, accuracy, endurance, strength and camouflage were attributed to his understanding of the manitou spirits

Collingwood to the Bruce Peninsula •

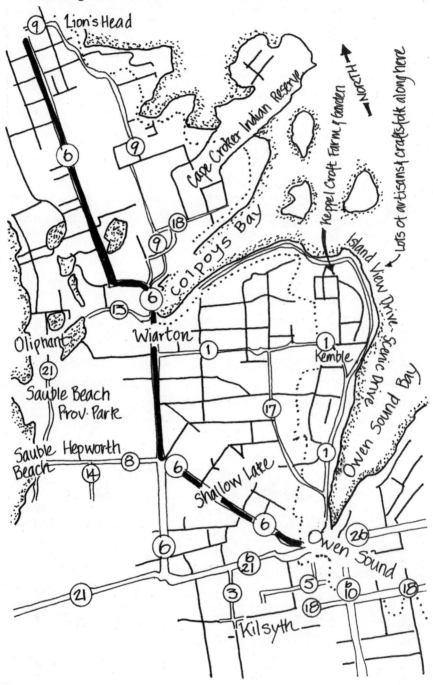

Collingwood to the Bruce Peninsula

TOBERMORY
Little Cove
Harmony Acres
Cyprus Prov. Park
Cave Point
6
Cyprus Lake
Cameron Lake
The Bruce Trail
Cabot Head
Lighthouse
Emmett Lake
Gillies Lake
NORTH
Dorcas Bay
Singing Sands
Larkwhistle
Dyer's Bay
Miller Lake
6
Colonel Clark's Tavern
Clark's Corners
Stokes Bay
Tamarack Island Inn
Ferndale
9

within himself. A hunter could boast about his skills hunting rabbits, pigeons, deer, geese, ducks and fish, without seeming vain because he actually praised the inner spirits.

For the Ojibwa, signs were present in the stars, in the flight of the birds, in an animal's appearance, or in the voices of the lakes and rivers. Signs came in dreams and in the prophecies of the shaman. Through his dreams, a shaman, or prophet, determined when warriors should leave for battle or hunters for the hunt. The shaman held responsibility for carrying the medicine bag into war. It was not an inherited position (though many sons became shaman like their fathers); a shaman had to prove his worthiness.

In the summer, the Ojibwa bands joined together to fish. One of the largest annual gatherings met at what we now call Sault Ste. Marie. During these gatherings, gifts were exchanged between bands, alliances were renewed, and hundreds of pounds of whitefish, herring and lake trout were caught. As the fish were brought in, the women prepared some for drying or smoking and the rest for a huge feast and celebration.

The natives of the 1400s still used the ancient trade routes mapped out by their ancestors. Copper from the west end of Lake Superior was heavily traded for centuries, and later, corn, tobacco, and fishnets were traded for buffalo robes and hides from the Northwest Plains tribes.

Fishnets and fishing remain important to the people of the Bruce. The first Europeans relied on the same food types as the natives. Though they raised livestock for meat and then traded for fruits and vegetables, fishing was the first major industry on the Bruce.

One of the first commercial fisheries was set up in 1831 on the western, Lake Huron side of the Peninsula. Captain Alexander MacGregor came upon the group of small islands we now call the Fishing Islands and couldn't believe his good fortune when he saw waters teeming with herring, whitefish and lake trout that weighed up to 30 pounds.

Tobermory

Georgian Bay

Lion's Head

Lake L.Huron

Wiarton

Owen Sound

The Bruce Peninsula

Sea stacks or "flowerpots" on Flowerpot Island. You can visit this island by boat from Tobermory. You can disembark and take a later boat back.

Bruce Peninsula National Park

A very diverse area, primarily composed of limestone bedrock it also has: sandy beaches at Dorcas Bay; Cameron and Cyprus Lakes; marl beds and ferns along the Lake Huron shore where orchids grow; rugged cliffs and caves and; cobblestone beaches along Georgian Bay where the scenery is spectacular.

There is access to the Bruce Trail through Cyprus Lake, Little Cove, east of Warner Bay Rd, Emmett Lake Rd and Cave Point. The terrain can be challenging so go slow, wear sturdy footwear and carry drinking water.

Captain MacGregor soon discovered the dark side of this paradise. The scattered remains of Ojibwa fishermen were strewn about the shorelines. The wreckage of canoes, smashed against the rocks or swamped by the dangerous navigation of these waters were everywhere.

Nevertheless, MacGregor went ahead with his fishery. A watchman was assigned to climb a tree on shore from which he kept a steady eye on the waters below. Sighting a silvery cloud moving swiftly beneath the surface, he shouted the alarm. The fishermen raced into the waters and encircled the school of fish with their gill nets. With the nets secured, the fishermen hauled them ashore, where a man in high boots spent his days scooping the fish, by hand, onto dry land. The catches were so large, a full net might take days to empty. Captain MacGregor sold 3,000 barrels of salted fish per year to a Detroit company.

Another fishery was set up off the north tip of the Peninsula where two natural harbours, dubbed the Little Tub and the Big Tub, helped to make Tobermory a thriving fishing village. Over a dozen commercial boats called the Tubs home into the 1940s.

The Europeans soon suffered their own losses to the currents, storms and cold waters. Known for its shipwrecks, the north tip of the Bruce is witness to the horrors of years gone by. Between the strong currents that force ships against island and shoal, fierce summer thunderstorms and the surprise snowstorms of autumn, these waters have wrecked many fishermen's boats.

Fire was another problem. By the late 1800s most outfits plied the waters in sturdy, stable tugboats fuelled by cordwood or coal. Errant cinders would cause fires. Terrified fishermen had a choice between death by fire or by water.

As the years went by, successful commercial boats and modern fishing methods provided many families with a good living. Although the Bruce Peninsula fisheries were no longer productive by the 1940s, postwar tourism continues to this day.

The Bruce Peninsula has something for everyone. The clear

waters of Lake Huron make Georgian Bay the perfect place for divers. Fathom Five National Park, situated just off the shore at Tobermory, is a popular place for divers to view famous wrecks. Bruce Peninsula National Park near the north end of the Bruce is popular with hikers. The rugged Bruce Trail, with its striking views of the Bay from the bluffs, runs the whole length of the east shore-line of the Peninsula. Small lakes and rivers abound. Botanists delight in over forty species of orchids.

Tobermory is a vibrant little town of shops and restaurants. Tober-mory feels a little like an East Coast town. Sit and watch the action in the busy Little Tub Harbour where water planes come and go, sailboats and fishing boats dock, and the *Chi-Chee-maun* ferry car-ries passengers to and from Manitoulin Island. On the shores of the Big Tub, divers explore shipwrecks and marvel at the plants and fish of the lake.

- **Picnic spot and hiking.** Consider taking a tourboat from Tobermory to Flowerpot Island, famed for its giant limestone "flowerpots" created by waves thousands of years. There are hiking trails, caves (ask for assistance), and examples of nearly all the Peninsula's orchid species on this island. Parks Canada offers guided tours.

Larkwhistle Gardens

North on Highway 6, just past Miller Lake, a sign points to Dyer's Bay. Follow the road east, and watch for Larkwhistle signs. Entry is free, but donations are accepted.

In creating the gardens at Larkwhistle, Patrick Lima and John Scanlon took our senses into account. Herbs grow among the per-fumed ornamentals; blues, yellows, reds and oranges play with the eye; the downy leaf of a lamb's ear and the powder-soft petal of a rose, the perfect roundness of a chive blossom. The full flavour of a freshly plucked mint leaf waits to be tasted.

- **Keppel Croft Farm and Garden** offers another great garden experience. Head east from Wiarton on County Road 26 to Oxeden and Big Bay.

- **Caves.** Just past Oxenden, you'll find the Bruce Cave Conservation Area.

- **Harmony Acres, Highway 6 south of Tobermory.** Harmony Acres packages hiking adventures and birding tours led by a wildlife biologist. In 1990 the United Nations named the Niagara Escarpment a UNESCO World Biosphere Reserve, ranking alongside the Everglades, the Serengeti Plains and the Galapagos Islands. The Bruce Peninsula is part of this unique ecological zone. Nearby Cyprus Lakes Park offers similar tours of forest, wetlands and migratory bird routes, with excellent cross-country skiing in mid-winter.

- **Picnic, hiking, and the freshwater tide.** Singing Sands on the west side of the Peninsula at Dorcas Bay is famous for its sieche, or freshwater tide. One of a few places in Ontario that has a sieche, this sandy beach is pleasant for a picnic in the dunes and a walk through the Dorcas Bay Nature Reserve on the north end of the beach. Parking and facilities are available.
The eastern shore of Lake Huron is one of the few places to witness the sieche. Nearby Tamarac Island (follow the signs on Highway 6 to Stokes Bay, then the Tamarac Island signs from there), with its magnificent rocky terrain, wonderful lagoon and rare orchids, offers an excellent view.

- **You'll find craftspeople, antiques dealers, and small shops all along Highway 6 and on some of the sideroads.**

Sawmill Ski Trails
  Hepworth
Suntrails Outfitters of
Hepworth sells day
passes at $2
There are 4 trails.
60% easy, 20%
intermediate, 20% difficult.
Classic and skate. Groomed
Managed by: Bruce Ski Club, Wiarton

Colpoy's Ski Trails. Wiarton/Colpoy's Bay.
Suntrails Outfitters of Hepworth sells day/passes
at $2.
There are 4 trails totalling 8 km. Groomed.
80% easy, 20% intermediate. Classic.
Managed by: Bruce Ski Club, Wiarton.

Rankin Ski Club. Red Bay
Suntrails Outfitters of Hepworth sells day passes
at $2
There are 5 trails totalling 18 kilometers. partially
groomed. Classic and telemark hill.
Managed by: Bruce Ski Club, Wiarton

Bruce Ski Club, Box 205, Wiarton, N0H 2T0
Season passes: $25/single, $40/family.

Sauble Ski Trails. Sauble Beach
$4/single/day. There are 18 km. of groomed and
track set trails. 20% easy, 70% groomed, 10%
advanced. Classic and wilderness trails. There
are 7 trails totalling 25 km.
managed by: Sauble Ski Club, Sauble Beach
        519·422·1405 or 422·3354

Lion's Head Ski Trails. Lion's Head
No trail fee. There are 5 trails totalling 12 km.
No grooming. Classic and Wilderness.
60% easy, 30% intermediate, 10% difficult.
managed by: North Bruce Nordic Ski Club.

Home to Home Route: Bruce Peninsula
300 km. of classic wilderness trails linked by
Bed and Breakfasts. Unguided though maps
provided when tour is booked. 80% easy,
20% intermediate.
Managed by: Ski Home to Home Network
519·793·3875 or 534·3901

Cyprus Lake Trails, Tobermory.
There is a $5 charge for parking.
There are 4+ trails totalling 10 km. No
grooming. Classic and wilderness trails.
Managed by: Bruce Peninsula National Park
519·596·2263

Recipes

Shepherd's Pie

½ lb sweet potatoes, peeled
5–6 potatoes
½ cup milk
1 egg, beaten
1 ½ lb of ground beef or ground
    turkey

½ cup chopped onion
½ cup wheat germ
2 cups green beans or peas
1 cup corn
Dash pepper
½ cup grated cheddar

Cook both kinds of potatoes. Mash with milk and whip in the egg. Brown and drain meat and onion. Mix all ingredients except potato mixture and cheese. Pour into 3-quart casserole. Spread mashed potatoes over meat. Top with cheese. Bake at 350 F for 40 minutes.

Zucchini Lasagna

2 very large zucchini, about 1 lb each
1 cup chopped onion
1 tsp. minced garlic
3 tbsp. minced garlic
3 tbsp. olive oil
1 16-ounce jar chunky spaghetti
    sauce (or your own)
15 ounces cottage cheese

8 ounces mozzarella cheese, grated
2 eggs
¼ cup chopped parsley
1 tsp. dried basil
½ tsp. salt
½ tsp. pepper

Bring a large pot of salted water to a boil. Cut zucchini lengthwise into ⅛-inch thick slices. Parboil in 3 batches, 5–6 minutes. Remove from pot and drain well on paper towels.

In heavy saucepan, sauté onion and garlic in olive oil over medium-high heat until soft but not brown, 6–8 minutes. Add spaghetti sauce. Bring to a boil. Reduce heat and simmer uncovered for 10 minutes.

Meanwhile, combine cottage cheese, half of mozzarella, eggs, parsley, basil, salt and pepper in large bowl. Blend.

Preheat oven to 375 F. Butter an 11 x 9 x 2-inch pan. Spoon a thin layer of sauce in bottom of pan.

Cover slices of zucchini, overlapping slightly. Spread ½ cup of sauce over zucchini. Top with half of cheese mixture. Repeat a layer of zucchini, sauce, and cheese mixture. Finish with a layer of zucchini and remaining sauce. Sprinkle remaining mozzarella cheese on top.

Bake in preheated oven 40–45 minutes until cheese is melted and golden brown. Let stand 10 minutes before serving. Serve with a salad and crunchy bread sticks.

Nutty Fudge

1 cup peanut butter
3/4 cup honey
1 cup carob powder or cocoa
1/2 cup crushed walnuts

1/2 cup sesame seeds
1/2 cup sunflower seeds
1/2 cup coconut
1/2 cup raisins

In a saucepan heat peanut butter with honey, blend thoroughly. Add carob and mix well. Add remaining ingredients and stir. Press into a 9 x 9-inch pan. Chill 2 hours. Cut into squares.

More Folk Medicine: The Magic of Fruits and Vegetables

Horseradish, thought to aid in digestion and liver function, and used to prevent scurvy in the 1600s, contains vitamin C.

An easy cure for insomnia is a combination of two tablespoons of honey (the darker the better), the juice of one lemon, and half a glass of warm water.

By placing a slice of cucumber over each eye, you can soothe away mental and physical irritations.

Garlic, rubbed on the body, is an effective insect repellent.

BED AND BREAKFAST DIRECTORY

BEAVER VALLEY

Glennkaren B&B
By the Bay
Glenn & Karen Naish
Box 613
Thornbury, ON
N0H 2P0
519-599-2186

Golden Apple B&B
Carol Blasdale & Arlene
McDermott
78 Bruce St. S
Thornbury, ON
N0H 2P0
519-599-3850

Grape Grange
Nan & Don Maitland
Box 39
Clarksburg, ON
N0H 1J0
519-599-2601

Hillside B&B
c/o Karen & Norm Stewart
Box 72
Clarksburg, ON
N0H 1J0

Rosewood B&B
Rosemary & Brian Barnett
R.R. 2 (Highway 26)
Clarksburg, ON
N0H 1J0
519-599-5285

Ravenna B&B
At the Ravenna General Store
Rosemary & Larry Morton
General Delivery
Ravenna, ON
N0H 2E0
519-599-2796

MEAFORD

Cheshire Cat
Joan & Doug Allan
32 Nelson St. E.
Meaford, ON
N4L 1N6
519-538-3487

Irish Mountain B&B Inn
John & Roberta Avery
RR 1
Meaford, ON
N4L 1W5
519-538-2803

COLLINGWOOD

Beild House Country Inn
64 Third St.
Collingwood, ON
L9Y 1K5
705-444-1522
Fax 444-2394
1-888-32-BEILD
www.beildhouse.com

Poplar Country Inn
R.R. 1
Collingwood, ON
L9V 3Y9
705-445-9592

**Pretty River Valley Country
Inn**
R.R. 1
Nottawa, ON
L0M 1P0
705-445-7598

WASAGA BEACH

Deerview B&B
Box 12
Wasaga Beach, ON
L0L 2P0
705-429-6498

WIARTON

Long Lane B&B
Joanne & M. J. Veerman
R.R. 2
Wiarton, ON
N0H 2T0
519-534-3901
fax 534-3901
Tobermory

Dogwood Point B&B
Libby Buchanan & Allen Potvin
R.R. 1
97 Eagle Rd.
Tobermory, ON
N0H 2R0
519-596-2671

STOKES BAY

Tamarac Island Inn
Bev Matheson
240 Tamarac Rd.
Stokes Bay, ON
N0H 2M0
519-592-5810
fax 592-5810

WYEBRIDGE

The Hackney Horse B&B
R.R. 1
38 Darby Rd.
Wyebridge, ON
L0K 2E0

OWEN SOUND

West Winds B&B
Ron & Mickey Breadner
R.R. 3
Owen Sound, ON
N4K 5N5
519-376-9003

Brae Briar "The Quilt House"
980 3rd Ave W
Owen Sound, ON
N4K 4P6
519-371-0025
E-mail dyuleos @ log.on.ca

MIDLAND

Trails End
Graham & Carol MacDonald
45 Blueberry Marsh Rd.
R.R. 1
Midland, ON
L4R 4K3
705-835-2158

Mark & Margie's B&B
670 Hugel Ave
Midland, ON
L4R 1W9
705-526-4441
fax 526-4426
E-mail mcoulter @ sympatico.ca

KIMBERLEY

Inn in the Valley
Box 34
Kimberley, ON
N0C 1G0
519-599-5099
Glen & Debbie Wilson

INDEX

OTHER ATTRACTIONS